Praise for

Before You Split

"Toni has given us an open, raw, and vulnerable look at marriage. This book is as real as it gets. She has not glazed over or discounted the hard parts, and she has not exaggerated the celebrations. She doesn't give us a prescription to fix our marriages but rather a path to honesty and growth. You will find in these pages a message laced with hope and filled with a challenge to get real about what you want in your marriage, why you want it, and what you're going to do about it."

—Bob Goff, *New York Times* bestselling author of
Love Does and *Everybody Always*

"I don't like when perfect couples write perfect books about their perfect marriages. It feels discouraging, unattainable, and, above all, fake. I want real books about real marriages that offer real hope. That's why I love Toni Nieuwhof's *Before You Split*. She offers practical guidance and time-tested advice to make it through the messy middle while building the marriage you've always wanted. If you've ever thought, *I wonder what it would take to make my marriage awesome,* then read this book."

—Jon Acuff, *New York Times* bestselling author of
Finish: Give Yourself the Gift of Done

"If you're stuck in your marriage or know someone who is, *Before You Split* is the practical help you're looking for. Toni Nieuwhof is not only someone we trust personally, but she's also a voice that needs to be heard when more couples than ever find themselves struggling in ways they never expected."

—MARK BATTERSON, *New York Times* bestselling author of *The Circle Maker* and lead pastor of National Community Church

"*Before You Split* is a unique and wonderful gift to marriage. Toni's clear-eyed experience as a divorce attorney, her vulnerability about her own marriage, her familiarity with marital research, her spiritual sensitivity, and her wonderful writing voice make this unlike any book on the subject we know. We cannot imagine a marriage (or life) that would not benefit from this book."

—JOHN AND NANCY ORTBERG, authors and speakers

"*Before You Split* blends hard-earned wisdom from Toni's own marriage with professional experience to create the essential message that all struggling couples must hear: what you are living today in your marriage is not your inevitable future. This book meets you in places of despair, conflict fatigue, and hopelessness, and offers you a lifeline—a practical road map that will help you pull back the curtain of your marriage, expose the roots of repeated conflicts, and challenge your hearts to move from a place of defeat and self-protection to hope and possibility. The principles in *Before You Split* have the power to carry your marriage far beyond survival into a place primed for the restoration of intimacy and partnership. From the perspective of a psychologist who helps many couples navigate marriage restoration, I urge you to read this book to help you make the best decision you can for the future of your relationship—one not rooted in emotion alone but in wisdom."

—CHARITY BYERS, PhD, executive director of Blessing Ranch Ministries

"Toni Nieuwhof offers us truth that is both practical and profound. This book is filled with real-life tensions that every married person has had to live with and genuine solutions that Toni has found through her vast experience and personal struggle. It's authentic, practical, applicable, and useful for every couple who wants to live their best life together. I'm so grateful Toni has chosen vulnerability and honesty as weapons of hope. Her words fight back against the despair of distance that threatens all our relationships. This book is a must-read for everyone in a lifelong relationship!"

—DANIELLE STRICKLAND, international speaker, advocate, and author of *Better Together: How Women and Men Can Heal the Divide and Transform the Future*

"Toni Nieuwhof is the guide you've been waiting for. Deeply wise, genuinely empathetic, and uncommonly insightful, Toni is a fresh voice with tried and true experience that offers a proven roadmap. Before you even think about splitting—split this book open and find the hope you've been looking for."

—ANN VOSKAMP, *New York Times* bestselling author of *The Broken Way* and *One Thousand Gifts*

"Toni Nieuwhof is a quiet storm—a brilliant mix of intellect, compassion, and revolution. Her new book is sure to revolutionize your marriage."

—SAM COLLIER, international speaker and author of *A Greater Story*

"I have never read a marriage book like this one! Toni's perspective as a divorce lawyer is so unique and extremely helpful to all marriages, not just those in trouble. It's an amazing and helpful book that gets at the heart of a healthy marriage through both practical tips and relatable stories. As a pastor, I have already recommended it to many couples and have assigned it as mandatory reading for those I am counseling. God is going to use this book to save marriages! Thank you, Toni, for sharing decades of experience and thinking with the rest of us!"

—MARK CLARK, senior pastor of Village Church, and author of *The Problem of God* and *The Problem of Jesus*

before you split

before you split

split

FIND WHAT YOU *REALLY* WANT FOR
THE FUTURE OF YOUR MARRIAGE

toni nieuwhof

WATERBROOK

Published in the United States by WaterBrook, an imprint of Random House, a division of Penguin Random House LLC.

WaterBrook® and its deer colophon are registered trademarks of Penguin Random House LLC.

Library of Congress Cataloging-in-Publication Data
Names: Nieuwhof, Toni, author.
Title: Before you split : find what you really want for the future of your marriage / Toni Nieuwhof.
Description: First edition. | [Colorado Springs] : WaterBrook, [2021] | Includes bibliographical references.
Identifiers: LCCN 2020014488 | ISBN 9780525653363 (trade paperback) | ISBN 9780525653370 (ebook)
Subjects: LCSH: Marriage. | Divorce. | Marriage counseling. | Couples—Counseling of.
Classification: LCC HQ734 .N64 2021 | DDC 306.81—dc23
LC record available at https://lccn.loc.gov/2020014488

Printed in the United States of America on acid free paper

waterbrookmultnomah.com

9 8 7 6 5 4 3 2 1

First Edition

SPECIAL SALES
Most WaterBrook books are available at special quantity discounts when purchased in bulk by corporations, organizations, and special-interest groups. Custom imprinting or excerpting can also be done to fit special needs. For information, please email specialmarketscms@penguinrandomhouse.com.

To my husband, Carey, for fighting for my heart and never giving up. You've made staying together a joy, and I'm right where I want to be: heart intertwined with yours, passionately in love, and once again completely smitten after more than thirty years.

contents

PART 3: TOWARD YOUR WAY BETTER FUTURE

note to reader

The stories I share from my years as a lawyer are composites and represent the themes of what I've seen in many families, where the facts and experiences of those involved were similar. If you think you know a man or woman from the descriptions in this book, I promise you it's purely coincidental and you don't.

I've used the terms *marriage, wife,* and *husband,* yet in doing so, I am not commenting on or making value judgments about your particular form of long-term relationship. I intend for these messages to help anyone who is in an unhappy relationship and searching for what to do next.

Please be aware that the legal consequences of splitting up vary from jurisdiction to jurisdiction and may differ depending on whether you are married or living together. Yes, I am a lawyer by training, but in this book I do not provide any legal advice about separating from your partner. If you are considering this option, you owe it to yourself to consult with a divorce attorney or family lawyer in your municipality to get personal advice for you and your family.

is your marriage harmful?

Maybe you find yourself in an *unhappy* marriage, which describes most couples I saw while practicing family law. Maybe you're unhappy because you've drifted apart from your spouse, you've lost the passion, or you're stuck in what seems like endless conflict. Or maybe one of you has had an affair. For whatever reason, you're desperately frustrated with your unhappiness.

A *harmful* marriage is different from an unhappy marriage. How? Almost each client I spoke to said his or her spouse was emotionally abusive. In all the marriage conflicts I've seen, things get messy. People say things they don't mean or intend. In many cases, the messiness of their conflict turned out to be more mutual than they could admit.

When you're in an unhappy marriage, it's common to be confused about where your emotional pain is coming from. I heard people say things like "My husband stores up all his anger from work and dumps it on me when he gets home. He's always venting." Or "My wife gets exhausted being with the kids and starts drinking wine before dinner. Then she zones out and blows me off." Or "My spouse knows how worried I am about our finances but goes out and spends anyway." In these cases, both spouses are dealing with pain. The line between unhappy and harmful is blurred. The causes are complex and not easily identified. Is one partner drinking or overspending because the other partner is withdrawing love or avoiding intimacy? The root causes of both partners' pain may be more intertwined than either person realizes. The words and actions that come from brokenness may be labeled *emotionally abusive* at times by our spouses. And that's how many unhappily married people talked to me about their spouses' dysfunctional behavior. But I think applying the term *emotionally abusive* in this broad sense isn't helpful.

Having said that, you need to be honest with yourself and take appropriate steps when your partner's words and actions are not just making you unhappy but are objectively and consistently harmful to you or your children. If your partner is behaving in ways that are violent or toxic, you need to protect yourself and reach out for help. Staying under the same roof with him or her may only cause you more harm. While that scenario I just described is pretty clear cut, for some married people the line between unhappy and harmful is not as easily defined. I strongly encourage you to seek help to figure out whether or not you are in a harmful relationship. Speak with a professional therapist or counselor to uncover why your marriage makes you question whether it's unhappy or actually harmful. At a minimum, talk to your doctor, a therapist, a pastor, or someone wise and objective whom you trust. Give that person full disclosure of the reasons for your concerns and take his or her advice seriously.

I know people who needed to leave their marriages because they had become toxic and abusive. Here's the point I'm underlining: I'm not advocating that you stay in your marriage, at least living under the same roof, while you're dealing with toxic, violent, or destructive behavior from your spouse. If this is your situation, please get professional help to make a safety plan.

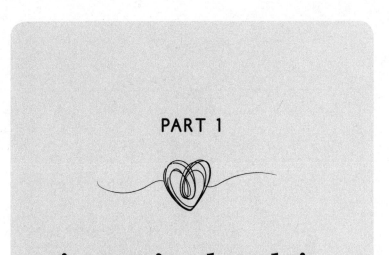

PART 1

i can't do this anymore!

CHAPTER 1

is there really no way out
of stuck?

One day, fifteen years into our marriage, we reached the tipping point. My husband, Carey, and I had endured years of conflict, now layered with ever-growing bitterness and contempt.

I was working a challenging job in legal affairs and governance for a hospital, and Carey was pastoring a growing church that demanded his full-time attention. Our schedules were packed with managing our careers and caring for our two children, ages nine and thirteen. Along with all the responsibilities of leading, serving, and volunteering at our church, we were involved with our kids and their school and all their extracurriculars, such as music lessons and team sports. Though our lives were full, we still tried to connect as a couple.

On this particular day in early summer, I breezed out of the hospital and into the front seat of Carey's Mazda. I looked forward to catching a lunch with him, just the two of us. The last of the cold bite in the air had been replaced with tropical warmth. It felt good as I breathed it in.

The lightness of my mood didn't last.

As soon as I closed the car door, Carey muttered something about how I had kept him waiting. My attempt to explain my tardiness didn't help. He criticized again. And in rushed the flood of frustration and resentment I had held back since our most recent unresolved argument.

Keeping our lunch date suddenly seemed futile. And I wasn't hungry anymore. Thick and suffocating silence hung between us. My hope for a better connection *this time* disappeared.

What was the hidden issue behind this argument? It went deeper than my being late. Because we had so many resentments, neither of us really knew for sure. On the surface, we had an endless supply of fuel for our disputes: who would be responsible for driving to the game the next day, who was cooking what for dinner, how the last discipline incident went down, whose family's event we would attend, who was working late that night, and on and on.

This day's argument followed the same old pattern: I would get upset over something Carey said and I'd shut down. Carey would respond by trying, progressively more insistently, to provoke a response from me. The more he tried, the more upset I'd become. The angrier I felt, the more I'd withdraw into my silent and zoned-out world. And then at some point, I would break the silence and explode into either anger or tears. It was as though this pattern had worn a rut so deep that neither of us could steer us out of it. We were stuck.

This day, it was impossible to hold my emotions back. I dissolved into tears. Head tilted toward the passenger window, I watched as drops patterned the sleeve of my navy suit. I looked at my hands clenched in my lap. Gripped with despair, I pulled at my wedding ring and forced it off my finger.

"There," I said, throwing the ring on the floor at Carey's feet. "You have it. I don't want it anymore."

Inside, I was a tangled mess of conflicting thoughts and emotions, desperate for our marriage to be anything other than what it was. I didn't want to be divorced, but I couldn't endure another hour of what our relationship had become. Unwanted anger, bitterness, and resentment filled me, but I didn't know how to get rid of those feelings. I hated being hateful. And I melted into one more self-pitying episode of "I just can't do this anymore."

Even with my thoughts clouded by anger, I knew the significance of my ring. When Carey was a cash-poor student in law school, he'd sold his prized Ford, the one that was a gift from his grandparents, for the money to purchase that ring. It was everything he had to offer at the time—a symbol of his steadfast love, devotion, and sacrifice. And now there it lay, discarded on the floor. That day, I was dead to compassion.

It became clear to both of us that something needed to change, and though the time for change had been many yesterdays ago, today would do.

how did i end up here?

How had my wedding-day dream of living "happily ever after" turned out *so bad*? And how did I end up *here,* writing a book about it? Not only did I go through a desperate season in my own marriage, but I've also learned from the struggles other married couples have gone through that I've seen from various vantage points.

I'm a lawyer trained in divorce law. Even before I threw the ring off my finger, I had a clear picture of the consequences of divorce. Perhaps I felt then as you do now—I didn't want to go there. Since the time our marriage was *that bad,* I helped hundreds of people through the often painful journey of separation, and I still do as a family law mediator. Being a divorce attorney is like practicing palliative care—only not caring for people through life's end but caring for people through the death and aftermath of their marriages. I wasn't motivated by any desire to help people end their marriages. On the contrary, out of compassion, my aim was to help people by ensuring their legal affairs were taken care of during a very difficult time of grief and transition.

I'm also a pastor's wife. Carey and I have spent several decades serving and leading our local church. Maybe you think being a church leader stacks the marriage odds in our favor. After all, we should know a thing or two about love, right? But I wonder whether it sometimes does the opposite. I believe authentically following Christ from a healthy emotional place does benefit a marriage. But if you're not emotionally healthy—as Carey and I weren't—you still get tripped up. Being in church leadership adds a pressured and complicated layer. We were passionate about serving Jesus but naive about love, and we lacked mentors.[1]

Much of what I have to share relates to what Carey and I went through. I was desperately unhappy in my marriage, and I didn't have a clue what to do about it. Since then, I've learned that the story I was seeing and believing at the time was not the full story. During our tough season, when I wondered if I should leave, I was unaware of how the emotional state I brought into our marriage was integrally wrapped up in the struggles and conflict we were experiencing. I had developed strong feelings of anger, bitterness, and resentment toward Carey, which had risen from our unending conflict. All I knew was I would look at our young sons and what we had built together, and I'd ache with the knowledge that I had to make a choice about what to do with all this negativity. And I thought, *It* feels *like it's over. So now what?*

Looking back, I know if I'd listened to my negative emotions, I would have taken my escape.

I'm grateful that I didn't.

what about you?

Perhaps you and I have something in common. Maybe you fell madly in love with your spouse and, for at least a while, you couldn't think of anyone else. You could have been surrounded with people, but your spouse was the only person in the room.

Fast-forward to now, when at times you can't stand being in the same room.

You may have found, as many couples do, that the spark that carried you through the first few years vanished far more quickly than you expected. Maybe you still have sex sometimes, but you're not fully engaged or interested in it. You aren't that attracted to your spouse anymore. Bad blood has followed you into the bedroom.

Maybe your marriage has you feeling overwhelmed. It's been tougher than you thought it would be. Your dreams on your wedding day now seem like someone else's. You feel trapped when you look at your old wedding photos and wonder, *How did we end up here?*

You look around, and your other friends seem happier than you are. You may have even spotted better prospects. The one guy on your work team seems to have his life together, and he's a lot kinder to you than your husband is. You're trying to dismiss the nagging thought that you're wasting your life by staying.

Maybe you're in that season of a long drawn-out argument. Or perhaps you and your spouse just drifted apart over time and the feelings are gone. Maybe your partner has changed so much since your wedding day that you hardly recognize the person you married. Or maybe you're dealing with the fallout from a betrayal.

How did you go from "I can't wait to see my spouse" to "I can't stand my spouse anymore"? Something has shifted so massively in your relationship that you find yourself thinking:

I didn't sign up for this!

I just can't do this anymore!

How can marriage be this hard?

This is not the same person I married!

My heart is breaking for you because I too have been to that awful place where I thought the only viable solution was to give up and escape. Even in the quiet moments when your brain comes up with reasons to stay, your feelings ambush you in the next storm, shouting, *That's it. I'm done. It's over.* I know the unhappiness that escapes words. And as real and as forceful as those emotions are, they may be trying to tell you something—something deeper than "I'm done." There's probably more of a story underneath your marriage angst than you realize.

Maybe you can identify with how I felt when I flung my wedding ring on the floor. Throwing off the ring was my way of saying, *I'm done with this version of our marriage.* We needed to get honest and seek help or we weren't going to make it.

Is it time for you to do the same?

Because I care so much about you and your family, I want to share with you what I've discovered as Carey and I worked through the messy middle of our marriage. What I learned is all rolled up with the insights from my work as a divorce attorney, service as a pastor's wife, and friendship with others who have had marriage struggles. When we found ourselves stuck, we had to get serious about being teachable. We paid close attention to the advice and marriage experiences of relatives, friends, professionals, counselors, authors, and pastors. The lessons for you and me are very real.

That's why I'm glad you've picked up this book. You're seeking one more chance, hoping against all hope that maybe something in these pages will help you fix what seems irreparable. I believe it's possible. I believe this because I've walked where you're walking and I made it to the other side. It was hard work, but Carey and I stayed together—and our marriage got better. Not right away. But slowly, progressively, we took steps toward each other rather than away from each other. And now we've been married almost three decades. I won't sugarcoat the rough years, but you need to know our marriage is sweet now. Almost thirty years after our wedding day, we both agree we are thriving. Could that become your story too?

holding on to hope

Carey bought me a new wedding ring. It didn't cost us a fortune and it isn't flashy, but it fits me perfectly, and I see it as priceless. It's a symbol of our better version of us, the one that feels fully alive. Replacing the old ring with a new one doesn't fully represent our path, though. It would be a better representation if we'd taken the old ring (which I eventually picked up off the car floor, by the way), melted it down, and fashioned it into a new one. Then the messy transition from old to new would be part of the picture. There were times when the reforming of "us" felt as though we were going through the fire and somehow making it out the other side. That messy transition from the throwaway version of our marriage to the priceless one may just be the most vital part of the story. We traversed a determined and, at times, painful journey that led us to the marriage that *does* measure up to our wedding-day dreams.

Hope sometimes isn't easy to come by. So I want to caution you about one thing. There's a danger in allowing the emotions you're experiencing right now to lead you to make long-term decisions. Yes, your emotions are real, and you need to accept them for what they are. Examine them. Learn from them. But don't necessarily give them the lead role, because there may be a story underneath your feelings, both for you and for your partner, that you haven't discovered yet.

You see, Carey and I struggled to take the first baby steps during the rough times. We had to fight against our emotions and decide to do what we'd been told would help. We stumbled, we fell, and we had to pick ourselves up and try again. I'm here to say it's possible for this marriage that you want to escape from to transform into a marriage you never want to leave. Your marriage can go from *that bad* to *this good,* and I'm here to invite you to see how.

Chapter by chapter, you will gain an understanding of what you can do to overcome unhappiness in your marriage and what's at stake if you decide to leave it. Through my experience in my marriage and the experiences of other people considering divorce, I'll help you see how to solve problems in your marriage and how to avoid some pitfalls if you split. Come with me through these pages, and I promise you'll be better equipped to save your marriage, have a stronger relationship, and move out of your unhappiness.

My hope is that you'll be empowered by the practical advice that will help you create a better story for your marriage. For you and for your family and, as you'll see, for all of us.

Why don't we get started?

FIND WHAT YOU *REALLY* WANT

1. In what ways has your partner changed since your wedding day or the day you started out together?
2. How would your partner answer that question about you?
3. What is your dream for your future together?

CHAPTER 2

"it's not my fault"

One particular summer day made history in our family's book of fun. While we were camping with our boys and family friends, we found a mudhole. But not just any old mudhole. The conditions beside the beach were just right to produce a natural, beautifully silky mud bath about the size of an oversized hot tub. And for our two young sons and the other kids who had discovered it that day, the mudhole was *the* place to be.

Why should the kids be the only ones to enjoy this? I wondered, so I decided to wade in to join them.

Eventually, our friends and Carey and I were immersed in mud up to our necks. Never would we have guessed we'd be sitting around, joking with our friends in a muddy pool, but there we were. One by one, everyone, coated in mud, left the natural spa and gathered on the beach, still laughing while we took photos to mark the moment.

As the frivolity died down, I looked Carey over. Being covered in mud looked cute on the kids—but on a full-grown adult male?

"Wow, you did go in deep!" I told him. "Huh!" Pause. "You may want to go rinse off in the lake . . . ?"

At the same time, he was fixated on me and said, "Okaaay, never seen you like *this* before!"

We both were trying to come to terms with how appalling the

other person looked. But did either of us see our own mud and think about how we must have looked? Not so much.

The thing about a mud spa is that liquid mud seeps into hard-to-reach places. When you immerse yourself in liquefied mud, it finds its way from outside places to the inside. Though we had fun, we had some serious cleanup to do afterward. Washing mud off your hands and feet is one thing, but what about removing it from inside nostrils, ears, skin crevices, and pockets? We all spent a long time in the lake after our spa. Even after that, I still found traces of mud in unexpected places during the weeks that followed.

This unwanted mud that holds fast in hidden places—the mud that found its way to the insides—may be a fitting picture for the first marriage problem we're going to deal with: our baggage and wounds and scars. You get immersed into the muddy waters of life whether you like it or not. The mud that finds its way to the inside of you may be the fallout from the hurtful things people said or did to you in the past, things that wounded you then and continue to affect you now. You may have picked up this mud at home or school while you were growing up, or at a rec center or a party—you name it. This mud is often hidden from view, so finding it and clearing it away can be a challenge.

Carey and I learned the hard way how much this hidden mud had the potential to wreak havoc in our marriage. During our rough seasons, I scripted a list of reasons why my feelings about our marriage were justified and a list of the things Carey needed to do to fix it. The only source of my suffering that I could see was Carey—*his* words, *his* actions, *his* behaviors. *His* mud. But it was so much harder to see my own mud. The mud inside me was staining my present, and I didn't understand how or why or what to do about it. And if I wanted to help my marriage—and me—get healthier, I had to find and wash away that mud from my past.

You see, the mud from your past may stain your present, but it doesn't have to ruin your future.

seeing what we don't want to see

Several years ago, my friend threw a party for her husband, who had reached a milestone birthday. This party was over the top. Catered delicacies covered the tables. Waitstaff dressed in black and white tended to the guests' every desire. A live jazz band marked the occasion. Party games and speeches filled the evening. And the highlight was the dancing. They even had belly-dance instructors who helped us pick up a new move or two.

About an hour and a half into the party, Carey announced he was going home. When I asked why, he said he had to install a bathroom light fixture but that I could stay as long as I liked.

My heart sank. I stood in the middle of the party's crowd and thought, *You're going home to do what? Why?* It didn't make sense. I felt my neck and face flush with anger. "What do you mean you're going home to install a light fixture? It's been weeks since we had a date night. This party's just getting started!"

"It's okay. You don't have to come with me," he said. "Enjoy the party, dance with your friends."

But my mood to celebrate vanished as the anger rushed in. I couldn't let it go, so I decided to leave with Carey. After hasty goodbyes to my bewildered friends, we headed out the door.

Once we were out of earshot of any guests, the tempest swirling in my mind came spewing out. "Are you kidding me? How dare you take me to this party and decide on your own to leave early! You're so self-focused. All you care about is your own agenda."

As we drove away, my accusations and anger gave way to tears. Our relationship had become shaky, and this experience made my reality even more painful. I was angry that Carey chose to leave our date night so early and that he was so nonchalant about leaving the party without me. What neither of us knew was that this tempest of emotions was the result of the mud inside me. My words and feelings in response to Carey weren't proportionate to what he'd done. Why? We didn't know it at the time, but that mud I was carrying around furnished a lie that told me, "I'm not valuable enough to be worthy of time and attention." When Carey cut our night short, he inadvertently triggered my emotions attached to that muddy lie. My heart sprang to my defense. My feelings raged against the notion, and I raged at him.

If you and I don't take care of our buried mud, it takes on a life of its own. And despite our best intentions, it begins to show up in what we do, what we say, and how we react.

As I continued to fume, Carey eventually told me the truth about why he wanted to leave. He was throwing a surprise birthday party for me that weekend. He figured he could let me stay at my friend's party and have a good time while he finished with last-minute preparations.

He hadn't intended to hurt me, much less send me a message that I wasn't valuable. But my emotions in response to his announcement quickly escalated out of control. The mud inside me may not have been visible, but the stain it left on our date night was more than obvious.

That's how it is with mud in a marriage. On our wedding day, we go to great lengths to look our best, don't we? The mud inside typically isn't visible that day. But that doesn't mean it isn't there. The mud hidden away in the creases and deep places only becomes more exposed over time as you and your partner do life together. It shows up in your emotions, words, and actions toward each other as you deal with your differences and struggle deeply to reconcile them. As conflict comes more easily, you see things in each other that you don't want to see.

Is it possible that finding fault for your conflict misses the point? Maybe the issue isn't your fault or your spouse's but is being provoked by the fallout from painful experiences in your pasts, hidden deep inside? Could it be mud on the inside that is, at least in part, responsible for your struggles?

what is your mud story?

I had a normal-looking childhood. My family and I lived in a nice home in a well-groomed neighborhood. My friends and I spent hours playing on the swing set and tree fort in our backyards and in the expansive fields and forests surrounding us. But where my childhood life seemed good, even privileged, I was at a disadvantage emotionally. I came from a family who faced life with a stiff upper lip, who did not acknowledge or talk about emotions or relationships. Authentic affection was missing. For my siblings and me, our lives revolved around completing tasks and performing well in school, music, and sports. And though I was a member of a family, I felt very much alone.

Our home may have looked calm and mostly well kept on the outside, but on the inside, it was anything but. My dad's uncontrolled anger surfaced routinely and worsened with his drinking habits. Intimidation was his approach to parenting and family life. When I mustered the courage to speak up, I was labeled bossy or was otherwise just ignored or dismissed. Most of the time, I didn't say anything and tried to stay out of the way.

Every day I walked on eggshells for fear of triggering the next tirade. When I needed help, emotional comfort, or support, I didn't turn to my parents. I found my escape wherever I could—in friends' homes and my cousins' home. I escaped into fiction and imagined myself as someone else: the heroine of the story or one of the girls in a sitcom family on television. I focused on performing well at school, gymnastics, and skiing, and I spent countless hours playing the piano.

At far too young an age, I threw myself into the arms of boys and the welcome relief of alcohol. Pursuing escape almost undid me in my teen years.

As I entered adulthood, I carried with me that belief that I needed to perform well to be valued. I attended a university and earned a bachelor of science in pharmacy *and* a law degree—and obtained the professional licenses to practice in both areas.

Starting out in my professional life, I had the appearance of success, but it required everything within me to control and hide how I felt. Several years into my career, I finally had to come to terms with the paralyzing anxiety and chronic low-grade depression that were linked to my past. It took a lot of exploring, learning about emotions and emotional intelligence, engaging in counseling, and praying alone and with others to expose the mud I was carrying on the inside. Progress was more noticeable in my professional life than it was in my marriage, which makes sense, since we hold professional relationships more at arm's length.

The truth is, I wanted to draw closer to Carey, my family, and my friends. But part of me resisted. It was second nature to hide everything going on inside me. As Carey tried to connect with me, my instinct was to keep him at a distance. I had become adept at saying the right words, using the appropriate facial expressions, and dressing the part to fit into normal, everyday life and accomplish what I needed to do. I functioned in my adult life as I had learned to as a child: keep my thoughts and feelings hidden and appear calm regardless of the circumstances. I really wanted a secure and loving connection between Carey and me, but I was emotionally unprepared to play my part. The deeply buried mud had distorted my capacity to engage in the emotional side of life in a healthy way. My emotional overreactions and disengagement were linked to the muddy lies, or untrue messages, I had internalized as a child, such as "I'm better off alone" or "I'm not valuable enough to be worthy of anyone's time and attention" or "I deserve to be invisible" or "My voice doesn't matter."

I've heard it said that "home is where you learn to love," but for some people, it's more accurate that "home is where you learn to hide." If you were raised by parents who were loved well themselves, you are fortunate. If you were loved well as a child, you're probably less inclined to mask your emotions or withdraw from others. You're more emotionally prepared for marriage. Trusting someone close to you will simply be easier. But if you grew up in a home where you weren't loved well and didn't have a great model of what selfless love looks like, you'll face a learning curve when you enter marriage.[1]

Your childhood may have looked different from mine, but none of us reaches adulthood without experiencing some sort of pain hidden on the inside—wounds, distorted beliefs about ourselves, and hang-ups. Carey and I have them. You and your spouse have them too. What is your history, your "mud story"?

If you're struggling to communicate or connect with each other and if you also have a tendency to overreact, stay detached, or hide or mask your feelings, chances are you've got some mud too. And it may be affecting your relationship more than you realize.

when mud is hidden, how do you find it?

My first clue that the mud from my past was staining our present was my overreactions. I had to admit to myself that when Carey said or did something that triggered my emotions to suddenly flare up, my reaction would go way beyond the occasion. And it wasn't his fault. My emotions and reactions were like trimming hair with pruning sheers. To sum it up in one word: *overkill*.

Carey and I were away on vacation with our young son when the first sign of inner turmoil hit me. In retrospect, we could trace out a few clues that something was off before the incident occurred. I was moodier and more anxious than normal, though it was easy to blame my mood shift on my early pregnancy. But one afternoon I was stricken with grief, which rose up out of nowhere. I stretched out on the condo couch and cried uncontrollably. I had this overwhelming sense of worthlessness and despair. I wasn't aware of any obvious, identifiable trigger. All I knew was one moment I was okay and the next I was clearly not.

For a short time, I was paralyzed in the dissonance between what I believed—that I was loved and valued so much that Jesus gave his life for me—and my suffocating sense of worthlessness. This extreme, despairing grief gradually subsided when we arrived home from vacation and I felt more stable. I realized that the crisis was behind me and I was still capable of doing what I needed to get done at home, church, and work, so I had a choice: I could ignore what I briefly saw from deep within and leave whatever that was alone, or I could take action to figure out what had provoked it. I felt compelled to do something because I'd seen enough of what was buried to know it was there. I just didn't know what "it" was.

I want you to pay attention to the clues your emotional life and your mental health have to offer. I could have spared myself and my family decades of discord and grief if I had faced my denial, dealt with my mud early on, and taken more immediate steps to improve my emotional health.

Carey and I were both good people with good intentions, but our love got stuck in our mud. I wonder if you may be in the same predicament. In your marriage struggles, do you find yourself overreacting? Maybe your spouse is saying or doing things that expose the muddy lies buried in you that tell you, "I'm not valuable; I'm not worthy of love." Yes, you feel hurt, and your spouse is the one right in front of you, so it's natural for you to conclude that it's your spouse causing all your pain—when in reality, the mud you unknowingly brought into your marriage is playing a role too.

Let's say the mud is there and it's not your fault. And let's say the mud isn't your spouse's fault either. It's been hidden away, unseen and lingering for a long time, perhaps. If you suspect that's true, what next? Even if mud isn't fully to blame for the brokenness in your emotional life or behavior, maybe it's playing an important part. So, what do you do about it?

you need a cleanup plan

My impulse then, as it still is now, was to ignore my emotional "red flags"; pretend everything was fine; distract myself with something, like a good workout; and focus on my to-do list. Something in me didn't want to expose the mud and its deceptive messages. I didn't *want* or *desire* to take the steps that involved looking inside. It was easier in the moment to deny that my own words and actions coming from that muddy place were partly responsible for our rocky relationship. Maybe you know what I'm talking about.

These days, pop culture encourages us to follow and nurture our feelings of peace. For some, leaning into pain is a sign of weakness, of being misguided, or of having a faulty worldview. Society tells us emotional pain is something to avoid. Unfortunately, this approach may lead to escapism. By escapism, I mean pursuing any kind of activity or setting that helps you forget your bad mood or negative feelings instead of trying to find out where they're coming from. I realized that if I wanted to stop my overkill emotional reactions and develop a closer connection with Carey, I *had* to look at that deep layer of mud inside me and do something about it. I needed a mud cleanup plan.

No matter how troubled or even chaotic your marriage may seem, you have more control over its future than you think. Regardless of what your partner decides, you need to start your own mud cleanup plan. You don't have to do it for your partner's sake. Your motivation? Simply to become a more loving version of *you*.

It's trite to say you need a plan if you want to make progress with your emotional health, but you really do need one. Here are some action steps that benefited me that may also help you make your plan.

FIND A SUPPORT AND ACCOUNTABILITY PERSON

Before you begin to discover and deal with the painful wounds from your past and the lies you've been led to believe as a result, you need a support person. You need someone emotionally safe whom you can share your self-discovery journey with. You'll know who this person is by the way he or she responds to you when you are struggling. Look for someone who is patient and kind, who is committed to having your back no matter what, and who will be honest with you. In other words, someone you trust implicitly. If you don't have a person like this in your life already, you may want to reach out to a mentor, pastor, support group, or counseling professional.

Though ideally your husband or wife will play an important role in supporting your personal-growth journey, you need other people in your corner too. I had a close friend I met with regularly while my marriage was struggling, and her wise advice and encouragement were invaluable. As we'll discuss in more detail in chapter 11, you need close connections with people beyond your spouse. Your husband or wife isn't designed to bear the weight of being your only friend and confidant.

EXPLORE SPIRITUALITY

My faith was an integral part of overcoming tendencies such as self-deception, self-condemnation, and emotional detachment—all of which were causing problems in my marriage. I gained invaluable insights from prayer and meditation, faith-inspired authors, and even inspirational music. Praying alone and with others led me to discover the deceptive messages that had been triggering my emotions and complicating our conflict. We'll discuss this more in chapter 10.

ASK YOURSELF, *WHAT PERSONAL PROBLEM WOULD I LOVE TO SOLVE?*

In addition to being triggered easily, I had another problem to work on. For more than a decade, I lived with angst because I had all kinds of ideas about how to make the world a better place but feared taking any practical steps. Even though our family life looked good from the outside, on the inside I was brooding and burdened and felt as though I was never living up to my potential. Why was it so seemingly impossible for me to pick a focus, make a responsible plan, and move forward? Why did I feel so paralyzed? During these years when I felt so stuck, my emotional state affected my closeness with Carey. My mud stained our date nights. Whenever we were alone, I would cycle back to the same unproductive conversation with him about how I felt I wasn't doing anything with my life, how I felt immobilized. These conversations were agonizing for him.

Once I did the work to replace the lies ("I'm worthless and invisible; I have no voice") with the truth ("I am loved and valued; I have a voice"), my emotional state improved and this brooding tendency disappeared.

Chances are, you don't have to look too deep to identify a problem that's been nagging you. You may have been putting more energy than you realize into suppressing it from your thoughts and attention. Have you already suspected you have a difficult time trusting others? Have emotional overreactions been causing tension in your marriage? Or are you struggling to lose weight, beat an addiction, or make close friends? Choose one thing to focus on.

ASK OTHERS, "WHAT IS IT LIKE TO BE ON THE OTHER SIDE OF ME?"

Have you ever wondered how others see you? Ask your spouse and perhaps one or two other people close to you what they think about the personal problem you've identified. Ask them, "What is it like to be on the other side of me?" This is a question our friend Pastor Jeff Henderson shares in his video series *Climate Change*.[2] Do those closest to you agree with your assessment of the problem you ought to focus on? What kind of climate do you bring to your relationships? Sunny? Warm? Cold? Stormy? When you ask others, be prepared for what you may not want to hear. Hearing the truth can be hard, but isn't knowing better than being in the dark?

EXPOSE YOUR MUD

Using the insights you've gained through reflection and feedback, start to explore the *why* underneath whatever problem you'd love to solve. As you do this, remember you are an immensely valuable, one-of-a-kind, uniquely lovable person—this is your foundational truth. It may also be true that you are stuck in your mud. So it's time to find that mud, expose it for what it is, and deal with it. Doing that will give you a healthier emotional life.

Let's say you suffered a wound that caused you emotional pain and while processing that pain, you started to believe a lie about yourself. Your survival instincts will have you bury the pain. But this pain, and any attached lie, lingers on and may be driving unwanted behavior or emotional responses. If you can identify the lie and replace it with truth, you can start to reverse this cycle.

Maybe one of the lies I've already mentioned resonates with you. Or yours might be "No one loves me" or "I'll never fit in" or "I'll never amount to anything." You may be able to identify who first spoke that lie to you, or its origin may be more mysterious.

Exposing the lie is important because when you do, you will be taking your first step toward your better future. Once you see the lie for what it is, you can do the work to clean it away so you can full-on live. And here's the bonus: a freer you will affect the trajectory of your marriage.

IDENTIFY ONE SMALL CHANGE YOU CAN MAKE TOMORROW

Once you've discovered a lie you've believed about yourself, you need to replace it with the truth. For example, I replaced "I'm better off alone" with "I need to rely on God and others to be fully alive."

Your renewed life begins with a healthier thought life, so start by making one small change in your thinking patterns. It may be to speak something that's true about you to oppose the lie you've been led to believe. Commit to speaking this truth to yourself out loud at least once every day.

But don't just stop at your thought life. After all, you identified a problem you want to solve. Identify one small change you could make tomorrow that will lead you in the direction of solving that problem. For instance, when I realized that I had been living with the deeply embedded lie that "I'm better off alone," isolation became my self-fulfilling prophecy. I needed to get out of isolation. I became aware that I had to be honest with my friends about what was truly going on in my life and in my marriage. I was keeping all the negative stuff private, but my resistance to being vulnerable with my inner circle only served to make matters worse. The one small change I needed to make was to be more honest with my close friends about my weaknesses. When a friend asked how I was doing, I had to be specific about my last overreaction with Carey and not respond with a flippant "Fine."

Whatever your one small change is, it must be a step that is doable enough that you could start implementing it tomorrow morning, it must lead you in the direction of solving your problem, and it must not require an excessive amount of your time, effort, or money. You're more likely to make progress if this one small change is sustainable and achievable.[3]

If the above plan sounds like a lot, remember that you can keep it as simple as needed. Pick one step to focus on for a period you define. For example, "I will find an accountability partner in the next two weeks" or "Tomorrow over coffee I will ask my friend what it's like to be on the other side of me." Break it down and take it one step at a time.

does cleaning away the mud really help?

When I finally faced the truth about my mud, I no longer blamed Carey for my unhappiness. And when I realized that sometimes his reactions toward me aren't my fault but arise out of his mud, I was able to be more compassionate. I can live out of the awareness that he and I are *both* dealing with the mud of our past hurts, and we are both working to clean it away. And that takes time.

How has cleaning up our mud helped us as a couple? There are many examples, but one stems from when I discarded the lie that my voice doesn't matter. While unaware of this muddy lie, I was internally fighting against it when Carey and I would argue. Our arguments would escalate because I wanted to make sure my voice was heard. And that subconscious internal battle spurred on my out-of-control emotions and overkill reactions. Once I believed in my heart, mind, and soul that my voice *does* matter and that I'm responsible for using it well, I no longer felt so driven to be heard. Now I'm better at staying calm, even under pressure, when Carey and I disagree. I'm by no means perfect at it, but I'm much more able to peacefully agree to disagree and search for a resolution we're both happy with.

Right now, you may not see the mud that you and your spouse dragged into your marriage. You may be experiencing the extremes of emotions that arise in the course of doing life together, even though the cause for your strong emotions may have little to do with your spouse and instead have a lot to do with what happened before he or she came along. From my experience, you can get out of a miry marriage hole if you are willing to invest time, effort, and even money to expose your mud and pursue personal growth.

Don't underestimate the importance of the choice you have. Only you can choose to search for the mud—the lie, the wound, the baggage you've carried from your past into your present. Your mud is connected to the painful words or actions of others that most likely took hold when you were younger and more vulnerable. To clean away that mud—to free yourself from the stain of pain and the deceptive whispers inside you—you need to find it and face it. You have to hold your feet to the fire, face the pain, and grieve your past losses. You need to get rid of that lie, and there may be more than one. If you will move through your pain, I promise you there is something amazing on the other side: a freer, full-of-life, and more loving version of you.

FIND WHAT YOU *REALLY* WANT

1. Do you ever catch yourself overreacting? If so, what are your typical thoughts and feelings when you do? How do your spouse and kids respond?

2. What clues in your behavior point out that you may have a "mud story"? How could you find out more about what these clues have to tell you?

3. Schedule a time to talk to someone close to you and ask him or her this question: "What's it like to be on the other side of me?"

CHAPTER 3

"i'm not being unrealistic, right?"

We were supposed to be in the car ten minutes ago," Carey said in his all-too-usual sardonic tone. "You're always making us late."

My instant reaction: "What? Are you kidding?"

Thoughts about making a last-minute run to the closet for beach towels vanished from my mind. In that moment, I switched from the composed mom who gets everything ready while answering questions and playing referee and cleaning, to the other me—the one who threw calm aside and took over, who stood with feet solidly planted and rose up red-hot angry, ready to defend myself.

"Where were *you* when the kids were fighting? I'm dealing with that while making pies for who? *Your* friends! And racing around to clean and get us packed up! While you spent all *your* time making sure all the blades of grass were perfect! And making your car shiny! While *I* haven't even had a shower! And you have the nerve to say I'm making *you* late?"

"This is typical you. Always behind. Never enough time," Carey said, his frustration now palpable.

Though there was a kernel of truth in what he said, it didn't stop the waves of contempt washing over me and the accusations rushing out of my mouth. "Who do you think you are? Ruler of the universe? Where do you get off?"

I'm embarrassed to say, but this episode ended with me screaming like a crazed fool and then slipping away into my own thoughts: *He just doesn't get it. He doesn't get me. I can't take this anymore.*

I cared, but I hated caring. The force of my emotional reaction reminded me I did care about what Carey thought, but I resisted thinking about that because his comments in the moment seemed offensive and unjust. I eventually slipped into silence and fought back frustrated tears, which felt all too familiar these days.

At this time, we were ten years into our marriage, and we lived in this emotionally messy, drawn-out tension, fueled in part by overblown or unspoken expectations.

We were both unaware of how much our expectations of each other were tripping us up. The problem was, we neither recognized nor communicated about our expectations—what they were or why we had them. We acted as if the other should just know them and meet them. As time went on, we both felt rising levels of frustration about not being on the same page, and because we didn't know how to get there, our frayed emotions only made matters worse.

I've seen many clients in my law office who also reached that point of emotional frustration or sadness and said things like,

"We're just two different people."

"I guess we're just not meant to be together."

"We're not compatible."

"We want different things out of life."

When the good feelings disappear, people tend to panic. Some people who said these things seemed to regret that their marriages weren't working out, but they interpreted the strength of their bad feelings as confirmation that their marriages were over.

But what if you instead saw your strong negative emotions as signals to dig deeper? What if your emotions are, at least in part, a symptom of an underlying problem? On the surface, you may feel so distressed that you're tempted not to care about what lies underneath. If you're overwhelmed by negative feelings, it's okay to admit it. Don't deny them or try to hide from them. But don't let them hold you captive. Do your best to consider the *why*.

For many couples, one of the underlying problems is unrealistic expectations. The good news is that once you recognize what is causing your emotions to fray, you have the opportunity to apply a strategy to resolve your differences more smoothly.

"we need a strategy"

A few years ago, Carey and I took a vacation, and I signed us up for sea kayaking. I envisioned us kayaking in turquoise waters in a cove or behind a seawall. So, the six-foot breakers forcefully crashing on the shore formed a new reality.

Despite my shock, I tried to absorb our young guides' instructions. To make it out onto the rolling ocean waves, we had to start on the beach and get through those breakers. We needed to duck through each wave and then paddle as if our lives depended on it. During a break in the surf, we quickly jumped into our kayak, and our guides on the beach shoved us away from shore. I swallowed hard and closed my eyes. I proved to be no match for the crash of the first wave, which lifted me off the front seat and onto Carey's lap. I heard the yells of our guides: "Paddle, mates, paddle!" I groped around for my paddle and desperately wrenched myself back to my seat before the next wave hit. This breaker shoved us backward against the kayak.

We wrestled with the waves and our paddles to carry out what we'd heard. "Flatten, brace, paddle. Repeat." Somehow, with no form or finesse, we emerged through the white-water breakers and onto the smoother, rolling waves. Riding the gentle ocean swells was fun, and the time flew by. Before long, I thought, *How will we ever get back on the beach in one piece?*

Our young instructors seemed to read my mind. They started patiently repeating instructions on how to bring the kayak in without being crushed by a wave. The underlying message was clear: applying a strategy was the difference between walking away or being carried. What emerged most clearly out of their advice: "*You* take the wave. Don't let the wave take you!"

It was a critical truth for us that day. And it landed us safely on the beach.

When I stop to think about it, our instructors' words ring true for marriage too. We don't want to get taken down by powerful waves of emotion. Could it be that to avoid being taken by the waves, we need a strategy? And if so, a strategy to address what exactly?

When Carey and I were dealing with conflict and our surging emotions, we weren't having honest conversations about our misaligned expectations. We didn't recognize the cause and effect. The emotions were obvious, but the source of those emotions was much less so.

Take the episode I mentioned at the beginning of the chapter, for example. We had lots of unspoken but clashing expectations. That day, Carey expected that he was free to tackle what he wanted to do outside and that I would take care of the parenting, the cleaning, and whatever else needed to be done. I realized after the fact that I didn't ask Carey for help that day. I expected he would somehow mystically see how I was feeling and offer to help without me saying a word. All my pent-up frustrations came rushing out when he complained about us being late—and then I was taken by the wave.

Troublesome waves of emotion arise when our expectations clash. I can try controlling those waves as they're mounting, but I know from experience that it's hard to do. That method is also reactive. A proactive strategy is better as it prevents the powerful waves from mounting in the first place: take control of your expectations before your emotions take control of you.

Adjusting expectations is a critical strategy. But to adjust expectations, you need to first know more about them.

expectations may be invisible

Everyone entering marriage has expectations. Most people expect to be loved and honored and respected. You probably expected to take care of your spouse and be taken care of. You probably had certain beliefs about what your partner should do and desires that you expected your partner to meet. The problem comes when we cling to expectations that aren't necessarily reasonable. In addition to the internal mud, most of us unknowingly bring unrealistic expectations as well into marriage. While the mud represents the unhealthy beliefs or embedded lies deep within that came from past wounds, the expectations are the standards or outcomes we're relying on ourselves or our spouses to meet or fulfill.

Our expectations arise from what we've experienced, learned, and observed in life from a plethora of influences. We absorb the messages from those around us, and as we grow toward independence, we form our own opinions about what we want from life. Our expectations are formed from what we've been exposed to in culture and media and in our homes, our schools, our friend circles, and other communities we've belonged to.

For instance, you may be used to your dad being passive and your mom being domineering, so you assume that the wife will make all the family decisions. Or you may be used to your dad always helping your mom without being asked, so you enter marriage expecting your husband to do the same. Or you may be used to your mom cleaning up after dinner without any help, so when your wife doesn't clean the kitchen on her own, you silently fume because she isn't meeting your expectation. Perhaps you see a messy home as a positive sign that you're living a fulfilling life, or you may see a messy home as a sign of failure. You may consider binge-drinking at a party harmless and normal if, say, your family reunions were always on the rowdy side. You may not have made conscious decisions to adopt any of these expectations; they are just part of who you *are*.

It's also true that sometimes our expectations are the opposite of what we grew up with. Someone who grew up with little is determined to ensure his family is well resourced. The person who grew up in a chaotic environment wants her home to be peaceful and orderly. If we perceived the behavior of the adults around us as negative or harmful, our expectations may represent standards or outcomes that are altogether different from what we were exposed to in our early years.

Whichever way our expectations were formed, we subconsciously label them as "normal." A couple runs into trouble when they fail to see how their clash of expectations are fueling conflict or when they fail to take steps to align those expectations. Since unrealistic expectations are often the root of the problem, let's take a closer look at how we can tell the difference between what's realistic and unrealistic.

realistic versus unrealistic expectations

In my practice, I've worked with many clients who struggled with their expectations. I saw the husband who lamented over his wife who refused to get a job when the family finances were under serious stress. I met with the wife whose husband seemed disengaged because he was always at work, dinner meetings, or the golf course. I met with many distressed spouses who were dealing with their partners' drinking habits. All these people had one thing in common: they were struggling with expectations, and for valid reasons.

A pastor who does premarital counseling recently told me about two couples whose expectations were both undisclosed to each other and dramatically different. During a session with one of the couples, he asked each person to write down the maximum amount of money he or she would spend on an impulse purchase without consulting the other. Once they each had written down a number, he asked them to reveal their numbers. One had written down ten dollars; the other had written five thousand dollars. They were both shocked. But on further inquiry, the differing expectations made sense: one person had been raised by a single mom, and the other came from a wealthy family.

In a session with the other couple, the pastor asked each person to write down how often they expected to have sex. The woman wrote two question marks. The man wrote, "Thirteen times a week." The pastor said, "Thirteen is pretty specific. How do you come up with that number?" The man was quick to answer, "That's easy. Twice every day and once on Sunday." The woman said nothing, but her eyes said it all.

Are all expectations bad? No. But expectations do fall into two important categories: realistic and unrealistic. For married people, realistic expectations include treating each other with respect, offering mutual support, allowing each other the freedom to be individuals, agreeing to disagree on nonessential things, and mutually committing to finding a way to resolve differences. It is realistic to work together to meet each other's needs.

Realistic expectations are achievable and over time will make your marriage healthier. They help you build a stronger bond with each other. A realistic expectation may include a mutual agreement that you both may access each other's phones at any time. Another realistic expectation is that you spend time with each other on a routine basis—with no work obligations interfering.

Unrealistic expectations, however, are the ones that get in our way, such as demanding to have the dominant viewpoint, meeting your own needs at your spouse's expense, prohibiting your spouse's individual thought and expression—any expectation that involves habitual lack of respect or kindness and lifestyle choices that harm your relationship.

Unrealistic expectations lack grounding in reality, wisdom, or achievability. If left unchecked, they will make your marriage bond weaker. Again and again in my practice, I saw overblown, unrealistic lifestyle expectations—such as spending without limits, failing to put boundaries around spending time with extended family, or making a career the top priority—lead to the breakdown of many marriages.

A common expectation is "My marriage (my spouse) will make me happy." Another one is "I will feel loved and fulfilled in my marriage, and if/when I don't, that's a sign it's over." But the truth is that your spouse can't make you happy. Happiness is something you bring to a relationship, not something you get from it. Only you can be responsible for your emotional health. And expecting to have the experience of unending good feelings in your marriage isn't realistic.

I knew a couple, Mitch and Miranda, who married in their midthirties. They seemed like a perfect match, but sadly, within three years of their wedding day, they divorced.

Stunned at how quickly their relationship deteriorated, I asked Mitch what led to the breakdown. He told me that Miranda was raised by a single parent and lacked any model for what a healthy real-life marriage looked like. She formed her expectations from what she saw on television and in movies. She thought her and Mitch's home would be organized, uncluttered, calm, and peaceful. She thought when they had a disagreement, they would quickly deal with it and even end it with a laugh. She thought their marriage wouldn't get bogged down by angry exchanges and frustrations. When reality didn't line up with her expectations, she couldn't reconcile the gap. Miranda told him, "I signed up for love in my marriage, not for all this arguing and negativity. I've made a big mistake." She bolted for the door and didn't look back.

In *Vertical Marriage,* marriage experts Ann and Dave Wilson addressed the unrealistic expectation of unbroken marital bliss. Many couples get married expecting continual feelings of love and excitement and become alarmed when they feel disappointment. The Wilsons explain that every couple experiences four predictable phases in a marriage. While the first two phases are characterized by romance and excitement for the future, every couple eventually hits the third phase of disappointment and disillusionment. What happens after that, during the fourth phase, depends on how the disappointed couple chooses to move forward: they either can work to overcome their issues or can decide their marriage is over. These phases may not be linear, and they may repeat themselves over the course of their relationship.[1] Knowing these phases are predictable, you can be encouraged, rather than discouraged, when you find yourself disillusioned about your marriage and your spouse. You can use that discouragement to figure out what's going on and make adjustments rather than give up.

Be assured that you should expect more than a few ups and downs in your relationship. Carey and I found ours distressing, yet those ups and downs were both normal and surmountable. Here's the problem: while it's easy to ignore expectations, it's almost impossible to ignore our emotions. And the reality is that our expectations and our emotions are linked. You can't ignore your feelings, but you also don't have to follow them out the door. Use your emotions as a signal, but don't allow them to become your focus. Instead, focus on the expectations underneath the emotions.

Research supports the concept that the best approach for expectations in a healthy marriage is to ensure they are realistic and neither too lofty nor too low. If you want to be happily married, it is unrealistic to accept consistently being treated poorly. Similarly, it is unrealistic to exist *only* to serve others and to neglect your own needs. It is realistic to expect to be treated with civil decency in general. We need to expect a sufficient level of respect, caring, and mutual effort to meet each other's needs.

Marriage research shows that for a satisfying marriage, realistic expectations are those that are "good enough." It's unrealistic to expect a human relationship, even a very close one, to heal childhood wounds or be the pathway to spiritual progress or, frankly, meet every want and desire. Expecting too much of your spouse sets you up for disappointment and disillusionment. Instead, it's best to embrace sufficient, or more realistic, expectations. Dr. Gottman said marriage expectations that are realistic look like this:

[A couple with realistic expectations] are good friends. They have a satisfying sex life. They trust one another, and are fully committed to one another. They can manage conflict constructively. That means they can arrive at mutual understanding and get to compromises that work. And they can repair effectively when they hurt one another.

They honor each other's dreams, even if they're different. They create a shared meaning system with shared values and ethics, beliefs, rituals and goals. They agree about fundamental symbols like what a home is, what love is, and how to raise their children.[2]

So, the problem is that when you're struggling in your marriage, your expectations are involved. They're provoking your emotions and making matters worse. But unless you put some thought into discovering the expectations at play in your conflict, they may stay invisible to you.

While the concept of "good enough" or realistic expectations may seem like a letdown now, it will lead to much greater satisfaction later on. It's easy to convince yourself to leave beause you can find someone else who will meet all your desires, but remember that this kind of thinking—"This person will make all my dreams come true"—got you here in the first place. And your next relationship, as wonderful as it may appear at the beginning, is likely to lead you back to where you are right now. Or, as some research suggests, you'll be *less* happy.

Is it possible you may be blind to some unrealistic expectations you have for yourself or your spouse? Just because none immediately come to mind doesn't mean they aren't there. Choosing to see them and then choosing to adjust them will require your resolve and courage. It's a critical strategy in turning around your marriage.

adjusting expectations

Unrealistic expectations, bad feelings, resentment . . . these words do a pretty good job of summarizing the pathway toward divorce for many couples. In my practice, I could spot the tension in couples who were moving through the steps to end their marriages yet were still experiencing regret. They were frustrated they couldn't make it work. They wanted that painful version of their marriage to be gone. They had lost hope.

Maybe that's you too. Let's say you buy into the idea that the emotions you're struggling with signal a deeper problem of holding unrealistic expectations. You're asking, "What can I do about it?" I have good news. There's *a lot* you can do. Let's walk through the steps.

STEP 1: IDENTIFY AND CATEGORIZE YOUR EXPECTATIONS

For Carey and me, some of our unrealistic expectations had to do with our finances. To say it was challenging for us to get on the same page with our money is an understatement. Ironically, finances were easier in our earlier years when we had less to live on. As students, our handwritten budgets seemed to serve us well.

Once we purchased a house and had other mouths to feed, our budgeting became more complicated and a steady source of conflict.

Having spent a lot of time throughout my life with my grandparents, who lived through World War II, I valued frugality and saving for the future. I held the expectation that all our purchasing decisions would be run through that same filter. But Carey's expectations involved being generous with our money and making high-quality, made-to-last purchases. Neither of our financial expectations were unrealistic or bad. It wasn't that I didn't see the value in purchasing quality items or that he didn't see the value in saving for the future. Our expectations became unrealistic when we refused to compromise and held on tightly to the idea that *my way is the right way.* That's when we found ourselves in drawn-out arguments over spending.

As Carey and I began to peel away the layers of our frustration to get to the root of our issues, we had to recognize the unrealistic expectations we were holding on to. Only then, as we identified them and classified them as unrealistic, were we able to take that important step toward healing our relationship.

Consider the areas where you have the most conflict, and look at each from an expectation point of view. Identify each expectation. Work on categorizing the expectation you've identified as realistic or unrealistic—but be forewarned that this can be a tricky thing to do. This step may be a process, so take it slowly if you need to and be patient. It may be hard to tell what's realistic and what's not, so you may need the benefit of wise advice to help you separate the two.

STEP 2: TALK WITH YOUR SPOUSE ABOUT YOUR EXPECTATIONS

If you're anything like Carey and I were, you and your partner have already had conversations about your hot-button issues and they've gone badly. So you may be hesitant to open up the conversation again. Also, if you're like us, there's a lot of emoting going on. Commit to having an intentional conversation that's different from the others. Set aside the time to have a calm, rational conversation about your expectations. Be prepared to be fully honest and to listen to understand.

Commit to doing everything in your power to make this a safe conversation—one that is respectful. Agree in advance that if and when it strays from civil, you will take a break and try again at a later time.

The point of this conversation is to better understand each other's expectations. That means you need to do some self-reflection first. You have to be ready to listen to what your spouse has to say before you respond. Assume that you will need to exercise self-control to not react negatively to your spouse's viewpoint. Don't use this as an opportunity to persuade your spouse of how right you are and how wrong he or she is. Your purpose is simply to share and learn without judgment. Be patient with your spouse, because this takes time and practice.

Once Carey and I started to really listen to each other and even appreciate the other's good intentions, we were able to recognize how our own expectations were unrealistic. That allowed us to work together as we both focused on how to adjust our unrealistic expectations.

STEP 3: REPLACE UNREALISTIC EXPECTATIONS WITH REALISTIC ONES

At some point, both Carey and I recognized that our budget expectations were unrealistic. Although it was possible for us to save three hundred dollars more per month and buy a used lawn mower (what I wanted), it was also just as possible for us to purchase the latest and greatest equipment and leave the savings objectives until later in life (what Carey wanted). But fulfilling one person's expectations and ignoring the other's would not lead us to a stronger relationship. So with practice we learned to develop shared expectations. There were times when we simply couldn't afford to purchase the lawn mower or car that Carey really wanted because our budget had limits. And I had to be willing to look at the family's and household's overall needs (and Carey's values and wants) and become more realistic about the dollar amount we would commit to saving for retirement. In the process, I had to address my fears about our future financial security. Carey made his concessions, such as agreeing to purchase a used car, instead of new. I needed to concede that saving for our future couldn't be the overriding priority if I wanted Carey to also be satisfied.

We all have at least one hot-button issue, and it's emotionally loaded for a reason. So I won't pretend that what I'm suggesting in this step is easy or quick. It will most likely be neither.

Your biggest hurdle in your process of replacing your unrealistic expectations will be more of an emotional block than a cognitive or creativity problem. You already know there isn't *only* one realistic expectation to replace your unrealistic one. In most cases there is a range of outcomes you both can be satisfied with when it comes to resolving your differences, and you are both called on to be open and bring your ideas and compromises. Your assignment is to release your ideal, unrealistic expectations and replace them with realistic ones for the sake of your marriage. It will likely feel awkward as you work through this step, but you may just end up being pleasantly surprised once you see results.

STEP 4: SEEK HELP FROM A TRUSTED OUTSIDE SOURCE

What if you still aren't sure what's realistic and what isn't? What if you get stuck? What if you feel your expectation is realistic and your spouse's isn't? Seek the assistance of a third party chosen by both of you—someone who has the wisdom, experience, and authority to provide guidance.

There was a time when I was bent out of shape with anxiety

about saving enough for the future. Carey's attempts to reassure me weren't working. But—and this is my caution to you—the strength of my conviction that I was right didn't mean that I was. Here's a case in point. Eventually, our conflict over how much to allocate to savings hit an impasse. No matter how many times we went back to the table with all the best of intentions, we failed to resolve this issue on our own. So we sought out a third-party expert to break the impasse. In retrospect, I should have taken this step sooner.

At first, we sought out a seasoned businessman who had demonstrated success in managing his own financial security. Then we consulted with an independent financial analyst. We trusted the people we sought advice from, and they had the experience and our trust to look into our financial situation and give us advice. We agreed to use their recommendations to guide us in deciding what was realistic and unrealistic. Long story short, I had some adjusting to do.

People often hesitate to reach out for advice, but even ancient wisdom recognizes the value of "many advisers."[3]

STEP 5: DEVELOP A PLAN WITH ACCOUNTABILITY

Armed with the insight from our third-party experts, Carey and I both adjusted our expectations and reached an agreement on the budget for our family. But we also recognized that because we had for too long held on to unrealistic expectations, we needed to hold ourselves accountable to the adjustments we'd agreed to. We were both careful to adhere to our plan for spending when we were making decisions. Then we followed up by routinely checking our actual spending.

Once we agreed on the basics—what we would give, what we would save, and what we needed for household bills—everything else became easier. We had far more clarity about how much we had to spend on the rest. I knew my need for financial security was met because an independent third party had affirmed our savings plan. I could more easily accept making a bigger investment in things like equipment and vehicles that were important to Carey. And he was committed to making sure we met or exceeded our savings goals every year. In short, the process we went through to adjust our expectations paid huge dividends in terms of our closeness to each other, our satisfaction in being able to resolve our differences, and our actual progress toward financial freedom.

What if the expectation you're working on isn't as concrete as a budget? What kind of accountability plan can you use if you're working on speaking to each other with respect and kindness? Not to worry! At www.toninieuwhof.com you'll find a template for your personal accountability plan. Simply fill it out and sign it to document your commitment. Keep it handy because it even has a place to jot down your wins!

STEP 6: GIVE YOURSELF AND YOUR SPOUSE GRACE FOR THE PROCESS

What is grace? It is a way of behaving that is acceptable and pleasant. And what is mercy? It is unearned favor or forgiveness. Acting with grace and extending mercy are essential for any close and lasting relationship because no one is perfect. So, when Carey made an occasional purchase that he thought I'd be okay with but I wasn't, the burden to relax the standard of perfection was on me. And when I gave Carey a gift that didn't even compare with a generous gift he gave me, it was his turn to respond with grace and mercy. If overall you're heading in the right direction with your plan, you owe it to yourselves to act with grace and forgive the ways you mess up from time to time.

STEP 7: CELEBRATE WINS TOGETHER

Once you've done enough hard work to experience a win, celebrate it. If for no other reason than because you owe it to yourself, each other, your kids, your dog, and your third-party expert.

How did Carey and I celebrate? After several years of working on reconciling our financial expectations, we made some special purchases for each other: a ceramic smoker for our backyard and a quality road bike. Once in a while, we splurged on a restaurant whose chef was from an entirely other food planet. Other times, we celebrated with a getaway to explore someplace new. The point is that you (and hopefully your spouse) have put in hard work to adjust your expectations, so as you make progress, take note and enjoy the accomplishment—whatever that means and looks like for you both as a couple.

take the journey to find joy

In retrospect, it's relatively easy to see why Carey and I struggled so deeply in our marriage. Many of our expectations were unrealistic. If we were ever to restore the good feelings we once had, we needed to have more honest, albeit difficult, conversations. We had to shift the tone of our conversations and be more curious about each other's feelings, priorities, and desires. And we had to proactively communicate about our expectations to stop being taken by waves of emotion.

Think of your journey to uncover and adjust expectations as a tour, not a speedboat ride. Remember, self-control helps, but being proactive about your unrealistic expectations helps more. Identify them, let them go, and be open to adopting realistic ones. Your payoff is greater intimacy. Andy Stanley, internationally acclaimed pastor and founder of North Point Ministries, made the argument that loading your spouse down with expectations eliminates the possibility for intimacy in your relationship. It's hard to have much intimacy with a person who is making constant demands or holding up hoops for the other to jump through.[4]

Having walked the long road of releasing our unrealistic budget expectations and replacing them with realistic ones, Carey and

I are now on the same page with our financial goals. We enjoy making decisions together about how much to give away and what places to explore on our next vacation. But even better than the financial freedom, we experience the joy of oneness. Every time we resolved a set of our clashing expectations, we shifted our marriage in a better direction. Now we're relishing the joy of a marriage aimed at fulfilling each other's desires and aspirations. Let me assure you, that is priceless.

FIND WHAT YOU *REALLY* WANT

1. On a scale of one to ten, rate your level of emotional self-control during your last heated argument with your partner, with one being "out of control" and ten being "excellent control." If your rating is lower than you'd prefer, what would it take to move your self-rating up by one number?

2. Think of your last hot-button disagreement with your partner. How much was your position linked to or influenced by your prior experiences, even your childhood?

3. Try to identify an expectation of yours, and spend some time thinking about the reasons why it is or is not realistic. Go to www.toninieuwhof.com for a practical tool to guide you and your spouse to resolve your differences in expectations. See if you can name three people you would trust to help you and your partner work through an impasse over whether an expectation is realistic or unrealistic.

CHAPTER 4

split, survive, or save: what do you really want?

Are you in the place in your marriage where you see splitting as *the* viable option? Or maybe you feel your marriage is stuck and you don't know what to do next. When you weigh your choices—leaving or sticking it out—neither fits with what you really want. When you move toward making a decision, it feels more like damage control. And let's face it, damage control is not inspiring.

Whether you're caught in an impasse or the spark is gone or you've drifted so far apart you believe there's no way back, you've reached a point most couples reach. In marriage, it's normal to find yourself feeling like it's over, whether that's for a fleeting moment or a season. And as we saw in the previous chapter, it's even normal to go through cycles in which you reach the point of feeling "done" but move through it and become satisfied with your marriage again.

Many people would say that once you feel like you can't do this anymore, you have two options: stay or leave. But I believe there are three options: split, survive, or save. These three paths converge wherever you are right now but over time will lead you to dramatically different destinations.

option 1: split

Splitting is an obvious option—one you may be leaning toward. There were times I leaned toward it too. I had a hard time resisting the impulse to run away from the pain I was experiencing. As a divorce attorney, I heard plenty of comments about the advantages of splitting: gaining self-respect, reclaiming control over my lifestyle and finances, having the freedom to move somewhere else, being free to start a relationship with someone else. Most couples I worked with in my practice wanted to leave behind the pain of their broken relationship. They wanted to close that chapter of their lives and move on.

However, splitting isn't as simple as you may think. Some people get completely blindsided by what happens once the decision is made. Take Matthew, for example.

Matthew's daughters were one, four, and five years old, and he had built his life around them. He was beyond distraught when he entered my office. "You have to help me see my girls!" he told me. "How did she get this order to keep them from me? It's based on lies!"

His wife, Ashley, had secretly obtained a restraining order against him. This order prevented him from returning to their town house and even from communicating with his kids until he had a court order allowing him to do so. Matthew assured me there had never been physical altercations or any threats of violence between him and Ashley or anyone else.

As Matthew and I gathered evidence, he showed me text messages between him and Ashley from the weeks leading up to their separation. I expected to find angry texts, but I was surprised that their words were respectful, even friendly. I did find a few mild disagreements, but nothing out of the ordinary.

This is it? I thought. *You're getting a divorce over what exactly?*

Matthew didn't have an answer. He wasn't involved with anyone else, and Ashley wasn't either, as far as he knew. Eventually, the story revealed itself. Ashley's closest friend had gone through a divorce, and what she shared encouraged Ashley to search for greener pastures. Ashley had some frustrations with Matthew, and eventually she proceeded with the divorce.

But why the restraining order? One can only speculate. In any case, their young daughters bore a lot of grief when they were suddenly separated from their dad, who had been there every day of their lives. Then they found themselves caught in the middle of their parents' court battle. This acrimonious divorce-court process went on for years, and Matthew and Ashley's working relationship as parents was seriously damaged as a result.

I'm not suggesting this is the scenario you'll face, but I want you to think about the reality that splitting up may get rid of an issue or two, but it will create other problems you can't foresee. Now that I've seen so many peoples' lives after they've divorced, I can tell you without a doubt that you're not leaving all your pain behind when you leave your unhappy marriage.

A divorced friend of mine reflected on his experience:

> Some people seeking divorce believe in greener pastures or believe life will be amazing. The truth is, it sucks. It takes a lot of hard work and a lot of time to build that new "normal"—particularly where children are involved. I wonder how positively different the outcome could be if the time spent dreaming about leaving a partner and moving on was invested in saving that relationship. After I separated, it took years to work past the guilt of what I had put my children through. People need to understand that you live forever with this decision to separate.[1]

If you have children and you decide to leave, yes, you sever your marriage, but your relationship as co-parents lasts for the rest of your lives. You may leave your marriage because you're done with your ex, but the reality for the vast majority of divorced parents is that you *can't* be done with each other.

I've also worked with a lot of clients who, after divorcing, told me, "If I'd known then what I know now, I would have tried harder to save my marriage." They discovered they hadn't actually signed up for better stories, just different ones. They hadn't considered that transforming their marriages was a viable option, and once the divorces were over, it was too late. While they did enjoy good things after separating, they wondered whether they could have tried something else to make the marriage work. They wondered whether or not the divorce was worth the problems it created. Divorce moved some people into a new reality that proved to be more painful than the marriage ever was. No matter how you've ended up where you are in your marriage, divorce is usually not an easy way out.

There's no way around it: splitting isn't going to look or feel the way you imagine it. I walked through divorce with many clients who were shocked by the gap between what they expected and what they actually experienced. They had a hard time coming to terms with it. If you've been married any length of time, and especially if kids are involved, even an out-of-court divorce will be harder and more complicated than you may realize.

Maybe you don't have kids and you're wondering whether you'll regret spending any more time in a marriage that feels broken. Couples with kids aren't the only ones who have something at stake if their relationship breaks down. Anyone who leaves a marriage of any length will face some heartache. Losing a long-term partner is often like grieving the death of someone close to you. Sometimes it feels worse because there's still a living person who reminds you of the sorrow. In the course of coping, it's not uncommon for people to deal with mental-health consequences, such as anxiety or depression, or addictions to alcohol or substances. Dealing with a divorce may drain time and energy away from a career or business. And then there's the financial cost. It's no surprise that divorce comes with a financial cost. If you've accumulated property during your marriage, your jurisdiction will have a formula for how it's divided. If your earning power isn't similar between the two of you, you'll probably deal with support payments. Obtaining a divorce involves legal fees, where the total amount generally correlates with the level of conflict.

Significant friendships and family relationships may be lost with the marriage breakdown. Divorce also affects our communities. We influence one another, and certain decisions have a communal impact. We'll come back to the importance of community in the pages ahead.

Aside from all the reasons I've listed, I believe there's a deeper matter to consider. Just as indifference and negativity influence us and the people around us, so do love and compassion. What if staying in this challenging relationship and facing up to your role in it will help you in the long run? I've met people who left a marriage only to realize later that they carried their problems along with them.

My purpose in highlighting these divorce consequences is not to say that the challenges of separating are insurmountable. In some cases, splitting *is* the option that helps people heal and move on to better lives. But we aren't talking about people in general; we're talking about you and your circumstances.

You have the opportunity to pause and look into whatever might be your role in your marriage struggles. Even if it's a small role. Maybe this is your opportunity to grow in your ability to love yourself and others well—*before* you split.

Is it possible that one of the existing barriers between you and a fully satisfying marriage could rest within your influence? Within you? You owe it to yourself to answer that question before you leave. Slow is your friend.

option 2: survive

What about this second option—surviving? Let's say you're both willing to hold off on making a final decision to split. Maybe you could survive in your marriage as you test out whether it's possible to stay together.

Henry and Rosie started out in the delight of romance and excitement, but after five years and two kids, they found themselves polarized by their differences and drifting apart. They survived their marriage for sixteen more years while raising their kids in their country home. How did they survive? Sometimes the tension between them would surface in front of their friends, but for the most part, they kept it hidden. Their sex life went by the wayside, and not knowing what to do about it, they let it slide. Henry stayed active in a band, played golf, and spent time with his friends on the weekends. Rosie belonged to a club at their church and frequently traveled alone to stay with her family a couple hours away while Henry took care of things at home. Implicitly, without actually thinking of it this way, they'd made a contract with each other to stay in their marriage. They were civil with each other, if not cool. They found some laughter and good times in other relationships. They each got enough out of the deal to keep them living under one roof. They stayed together, but their hearts were apart. They were in survival mode.

Surviving in marriage *does* have advantages. The pros of surviving may include stability for your kids or less financial strain on your family. Maybe staying in your marriage helps you maintain friendships or family relationships that benefit you and your family. But if your marriage feels like a business deal, lacking a real emotional bond, sooner or later one of you may end up responding to that empty feeling inside in an unhealthy way.

Here's the surviving equation:

Surviving = Staying Together + Emotional Disconnection

I recently polled a group at a marriage seminar. I asked partici-
pants to rate their level of satisfaction with their marriages. On
average, they rated their marriages a C+. The good news is, they're
not giving their marriages an F. The bad news is, these married
people are barely satisfied and they're not thriving.

A surviving marriage is a marriage at risk if it stays that way.
Long-term surviving not only is a poor strategy but may result
with one of you being blindsided. Being disconnected in this crucial relationship can cause a loneliness and an emptiness that are
powerful influences. Deep down, you're wired for an authentic, loving connection with the person you committed to. Without a real
connection, you'll feel like something's missing. Because something is.

Therefore, surviving in marriage should be both intentional
and temporary. This is what I invite you to consider: Could you
survive in your marriage as part of a strategy to save it?

Surviving may be exactly what you need to do while you and
your partner work on personal growth and learn to love each other
better. But make it your goal to *not* get stuck surviving.

option 3: save

When I talk about saving your marriage, I'm not talking about you
and your spouse forcing yourselves to stay together under the same
roof, carrying on with the status quo—especially if you're surviving. Instead, I'm talking about transforming your marriage into
one that makes you both feel loved, cared for, and fully satisfied.
This may seem like a pipe dream. You may want to experience
these things, but the bond between you is so broken that you aren't
sure how this can even be a possibility. That gap between "survive"
and "save" relates to and depends upon the strength and quality of
the heartfelt bond between you. How to move your relationship

from the disconnection of "surviving" to the authentic closeness of "saving" is *the* question.

When I was in that hopeless place in my marriage, I had a hard time thinking about the future. I couldn't imagine being in love with Carey again. One night after a heated argument, we talked about being done and separating, and at that point the potential consequences started to crystallize for me. When I thought about the impact this would have on our family, our extended family, our work and ministry, and our community, let alone the financial consequences, it became clear that splitting wasn't what I really wanted. I recognized that we had no guarantee of happiness, regardless of which choice we made. But knowing we were contemplating splitting gave us the incentive to set aside complacency and start making efforts to turn things around. We got serious and committed to marriage counseling. Applying the practical advice from our counselor felt awkward and took practice. Sometimes we avoided arguing in front of the kids; sometimes we didn't. When we succeeded one day in halting an argument before it got nasty, the next day we failed. But when we kept going, even with setbacks, gradually we made progress.

Now what we've found over all these years (and other couples have found too) is that we *can* build a fully satisfying and life-giving relationship again, even after the lowest lows. You can too. We'll look at some how-tos in the chapters ahead.

A wise group of counselors I know[2] agree that you can make progress to fix your marriage despite the bad feelings between you. Regardless of how much you're fighting or drifting apart, it's possible to turn things around. These experts say you need openness to take advice, courage to be vulnerable[3] and look inside, and willingness to try. Openness, courage, and willingness.

For Carey and me, being fully present, listening to each other, and accepting and responding to each other's emotions is a work in progress. During our tough season, we weren't emotionally safe for each other. Now most of the time, when we make the effort, we can reach a place where we both feel heard and supported by the other. We're not perfect at it—we still step on each other's toes. Once in a while, we even blow up like we used to. But both of us try to recognize when we're going down that old beaten path that leads us to nowhere good. We try to have humility, apologize faster, and own our mistakes.

Despite the imperfections, we both feel our marriage is thriving. And we're grateful we stayed together. Even after so many years married, we get a lot of pleasure from spending time together. We continue to have fun when it's just the two of us. Our shared history helps us support and give wise advice to each other. Our conversations are interesting and fresh. Our intimacy is joy-filled. We have shared dreams. Being emotionally safe for each other has helped us care more about each other's desires. Our marriage is a refuge from the harsh things in life. Our hearts are far more connected than they were ten or fifteen years ago, and we're thrilled that we *get* to be married to each other at our current stage.

This is why I'm presenting the possibility of a saved marriage for *you*.

what do you really want?

Even as I contemplated leaving our painful marriage, deep down I knew what I really wanted. I wanted to get rid of the painful version and replace it with a much better one. So, now I'm asking you: What does your heart really want? What do *you* really want?

If something in you says you may want to *save* your marriage, you may need to go through a season of surviving it first. That's okay. Emerging evidence shows that long-term romantic relationships have more to offer than their short-term counterparts. Researchers have concluded that among couples who reported happiness after ten years of being together, the dopamine-rich areas of the brain still fired up with romantic love. In other words, these couples didn't just share companion love but were sexually engaged and had bonds similar to parent-infant.[4] Maybe if you survive with the goal of saving your marriage, you'll find what Carey and I and so many other couples have—a satisfying and passionate relationship that makes you love being home together.

You may be asking, Is this even possible—when it feels like my dream of being happily married is dead? I'm glad you asked.

Researcher Linda Waite, along with a team of sociologists, studied 645 unhappily married spouses. She surveyed them at the start of the study (when they were reporting marital unhappiness) and then again five years later. She compared them in two groups: spouses who stayed together and spouses who divorced.

After the five-year period, 66 percent of the spouses who initially gave the lowest rating on the happiness scale (one or two out of seven) and decided to stay together reported becoming happy again in their marriages. Compare this with the group who initially gave the same low ratings but then divorced: only 19 percent of them reported being happily married at the five-year mark.[5] If you want to be happy in your marriage but currently aren't, chances are you might as well stay together. Your odds of being happily married in five years are better if you do.

So, despite the way you feel right now, what do you *really* want? I know this is a hard question. I was also skeptical about whether Carey and I could make progress. But now that our marriage is thriving, I realize that if we had split, I would have left behind so much good. And my insecurities and anger might have morphed, but they wouldn't have deserted me. I discovered that Carey didn't deserve all the blame for my unhappiness, like I had thought in the moment. And if you'd told me all those years ago that it's possible to go from *that bad* to *this good,* I would have thought, *Sure, for someone else.*

Salvaging a relationship is more complicated when a couple has hit the point of mutual contempt, and we were there. I was too bitter and frustrated to care much about Carey's feelings. But I worked on our marriage even though I felt like running away, because I cared about our kids and wanted to keep my vows. Working on saving our marriage was slow going, but eventually it paid off big time.

Your marriage *can* change. Dramatically.

What if there's joy on the other side of your heartbreak? What if there are real feelings on the other side of saying yes to a step?

Why not give your future self the gift of your best shot?

Whether you split, survive, or save your marriage, you will have hard work ahead of you. But if you split up before taking a closer look at how loving you are toward your spouse and how loving you are to yourself, you may miss the message that your relational crisis would tell you. You may find yourself a few years into your next relationship dealing with the same problems you thought you'd left behind.

In the end, which option is best for you and your family is your decision to make. Your spouse may reach a different conclusion than you do. The reality is that neither of you will be able to control the other person's decision. Though you don't have control, you do still have influence. Even though all you may be able to see right now is your struggling marriage, you may in reality have the opportunity of a lifetime.

All it took was a little bit of progress with one step to give me the hope and courage to take the next step. And the next one, and the one after that. A little bit of progress showed me the possibility of getting what my heart *really* wanted. Do you think it might be possible to take steps to see if your marriage can come alive again? Let's start exploring *how*.

FIND WHAT YOU *REALLY* WANT

1. When you think over the highlight reel of your relationship, which moments stand out?
2. Describe a time when you acted in a loving way toward someone even though the circumstances were challenging. Would your best friend say this is typical of you?
3. Do you know anyone whose marriage merely survived for a time and then improved? Invite this person out for lunch and ask what he or she did to make the relationship better.

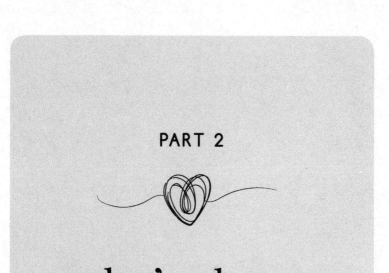

PART 2

so let's change
this

CHAPTER 5

how to move closer instead of moving on

In my law practice, I realized after a while that when people came into my office for their first meeting, they were in dramatically differing emotional states. Some came in with their fear or anger at an all-time high—having just discovered an affair or after having a blowup that led to the first real conversation about splitting up. Others came to me long after they'd lost their emotional connection to their spouses. They'd already gone through the stages of grief and made peace with the breakdown of their relationship but were still living together. They said things like, "We separated five years ago—he moved to the basement. It's been over for a long time. We just need to make it legal." They made it clear they had no intention of going back.

The couples who were more emotional were actually closer to having a real relationship again. When people become distressed and overwhelmed with the negative emotions stirred up in their marriages, they often don't know what to do with those emotions. Feeling disconnected gives rise to fears, such as the fear of rejection, abandonment, or being trapped in a loveless marriage. No wonder people have the impulse to run in the opposite direction. Our feelings can masquerade as truth and be the falsest of friends.

But experiencing the emotions of grief—such as anger, frustration, desperation, fear, or sadness—could signal that you still care enough to work on the relationship. As much as you may think your anger, loathing, and deep distress are signs that your relationship is irreparable, they're actually signs that you're still invested at some level. The opposite of love isn't hate; it is indifference. And if you aren't there yet, you may have more hope for a restored marriage than you think.

If neither you nor your spouse has made the decision that you're done, you have the option of taking steps to bring you closer again. What's important is how you respond to the negative emotions. Feeling disconnected at times or moving in and out of stressful emotions is normal for married people. So it's important to choose your focus. Your focus on despair or escape may initiate your future apart. And despite your feelings, you *do* have ways to move closer rather than moving on. I'll show you how with these three tips.

tip #1: avoid the blame-and-shame game

Have you thought about your relationship as a safe emotional space for you and your spouse? Emotional safety is crucial to keeping an authentic connection, yet this is a common blind spot. When you both feel safe and know that your partner has your back, you're able to move closer to each other instead of moving on, away from each other. On the other hand, there's nothing like blame and shame to make you feel unsafe. That's where this first tip comes in.

If Carey and I could each draw a sphere around the space containing everything we see as fun, our spheres would have little overlap. I find running to be fun; Carey doesn't. Carey leaps out of bed excited to wash his car on Saturday mornings; I drag myself to do that. On vacations, Carey loves to be in a vibrant urban atmosphere, whereas I love camping.

In our earlier years together, Carey once tried to appease me because I was so insistent about my version of a fun vacation. I knew he wasn't looking forward to camping, but he was being a good sport and taking one for the team. Since we weren't avid campers, we didn't own any gear other than sleeping bags. When our friends generously offered to loan us their equipment, from tents to pots to a camp stove, I eagerly accepted. We piled all of it into our station wagon, and Carey, the kids, and I headed north.

After a few hours of fumbling to get the rods connected and the pegs into the ground—and an earful of grumbling—we had the campsite set up. A tent for the kids, a tent for Carey and me, and a kitchen tent to enclose all our food supplies. And just in time—the sky was growing gray and darker by the moment, even though it was just midafternoon. Carey and I stretched out side by side on our sleeping bags and listened as the rain splattered off the tent roof. Carey flinched when a raindrop hit his forehead, and then he scowled. "I knew this was a bad idea," he said. We watched the rain slowly soak the roof, then drip its way through.

I still clung to my optimism and suggested that we move ourselves and all our things into the dry kitchen tent to wait out the storm, which we did. But heavy rainfall went on for hours and showed no signs of abating.

Later, as ominous clouds disappeared into the blackness of night and the torrents of rain worsened, a half barrel of water weighed down the roof of the kitchen tent. The roof resembled an old horse with a curved back and massively oversized stomach. Carey tried to relieve the tent by pushing it up in the middle but only succeeded in releasing the waterfall over himself, our food, and our supplies. Everything was soaked, including our sleeping bags.

"That's it. I'm not sleeping here," he said. "I'm driving home, getting a good night's sleep in a dry bed, and coming back in the morning. Then I'll clean up this mess."

"What do you mean you're bailing on our vacation?" I asked, my temper escalating. "You never wanted to come on this vacation in the first place! All you ever think about is yourself and your own comfort. It doesn't even cross your mind how much work I put into gathering up all this equipment, cleaning it, packing everything. I spent two weeks getting us ready for this trip. I knew you would do this—you always ruin anything I want to do."

The truth was that Carey hadn't ruined our vacation. I hadn't checked whether our tents were actually waterproof. That was my first mistake. I had also failed to check the weather forecast. If I had, we would have been better prepared. But at the height of my frustration, I rushed to blame Carey.

When I fall into the blame-and-shame trap, I move into my invisible fortress and start shooting arrows at Carey. It doesn't matter if he's at fault or not. I lash out without rationally thinking or considering his perspective. In blame-and-shame mode, I don't think about how my words and actions may hurt him and tear down our relationship. As much as I hate to admit it, I've done it again and again. Maybe you have too?

Blame and shame, aim and maim. It isn't pretty, and there are no winners.

A dead giveaway for when Carey and I were playing the blame-and-shame game was the language we'd use: "You always . . ." or "You never . . ." We'd get stuck in patterns, playing them out over and over again. What I didn't understand then is that words have power. There are no neutral or empty words. The words we speak to our spouses and to ourselves will either build up or tear down. That means we have to choose our words carefully. We need to pause and reflect before we speak.

My marriage with Carey is thriving now, but it wouldn't be if he and I hadn't made a conscious decision to stop blaming each other. Our counselor helped each of us see the pattern of blame and shame we had unwittingly fallen into. He helped us to stop focusing on what we were blaming each other for and to start focusing more constructively on our responses and self-control.

While there's no easy formula for breaking a blame-and-shame pattern, being aware of it and feeling motivated to break the pattern is a first and very important step. Recognizing your body's clues that you're losing your self-control is also crucial.

For instance, if an argument between Carey and me is getting heated, I may start to feel anxious or fearful and my hands and feet may become cold. As my anger rises, I may feel my heart start to race. I begin to perspire. My thinking becomes clouded. This is my body's fight-or-flight reaction kicking in. And if I don't pay attention to these signs when they first appear, then I more easily fall into the blame-and-shame game and am more prone to lash out.

I like the way a physician friend explains these warning signs to his patients. He tells them to pay attention to whether their emotional status is in the green, yellow, or red zone. Green is calm and cool. Red is the emotionally triggered zone I described above, where heightened emotions take over. The yellow zone is somewhere in between.

Reaching the red zone is a definite signal that whatever exchange or argument you're involved in needs to stop. This is the zone where you're at a much higher risk of saying or doing something you'll later regret, since it's no longer possible to think calmly and rationally. Make it your goal to air your differences, especially the ones that provoke your emotions, only when you both can start in the green zone, cool and clearheaded.

Here are other techniques to help you avoid the blame-and-shame game:

- If you notice your emotions heading to the yellow zone, stop, breathe deeply, and start speaking again with a calm tone. Your own calm voice can have a soothing effect on yourself.

- Ask why. Have an attitude of curiosity. Ask your spouse to explain his or her motives or intentions—and watch your tone so you don't sound judgmental. Then listen carefully.

- Talk about how you feel. Instead of saying, "You always . . ." or "You never . . . ," just say, "I feel hurt when you say . . ."

- Allow for natural consequences when they don't put anyone at risk. Your spouse needs a partner, not a parent. For example, rather than blaming your spouse for driving too fast or aggressively, simply don't say anything and allow the natural consequences to happen, such as getting a speeding ticket or demerit points. (If you're concerned that the natural consequences may put you at risk, reach out to someone wise and ask for his or her perspective.)

- Shift your focus from your spouse ("*You* did" or "*You* said" or "*You* didn't") to yourself. Ask yourself, *How did I contribute to this disagreement?*

- Be responsible for your own emotions and self-control. If you find your sadness, anxiety, or anger seems to come from a deep well, then the cause probably isn't only your spouse. In other words, your spouse is not solely to blame. Love and joy aren't emotions you take from your partner; they are emotions you bring.

- Work on having empathy. Stay in the moment to accept your spouse's emotions for what they are and avoid judgment. I'll talk more about this in the next section.

I know from experience that making these shifts is not like following a recipe. If blame has been an issue between the two of you, the way out is messy. Sometimes you'll remember to stop, ask, and listen, and sometimes you won't. One morning you'll recognize your impulse to point blame and you'll stop yourself before you do, and later when you're feeling worn out, you'll slip up. Just keep at it. Since Carey and I gradually learned to apply these techniques, we have an easier time facing difficulties together. Take, for example, what happened a few months ago in our driveway.

We'd just returned from an out-of-town conference. After a long flight, we were both exhausted, and it was close to midnight. Carey was driving us home in my car, and as he backed it into our driveway, we heard a crash as the car lurched to a stop. There was only one other vehicle in our spacious driveway—his. It took a second for it to sink in. He had backed my car into his.

Years ago, this would have ignited an argument that would have smoldered for days. My knee-jerk reaction would have been "Why didn't you slow down? Why can't you be more careful?" Instead, because we had been working on ditching blame, the scene played out differently. Now my emotions responded to his. My automatic response was empathy, not blame. It was an accident, and no doubt Carey was frustrated that he'd backed my car into his. So I said, "Oh, Carey, I'm sorry." (Even though there was nothing for me to be sorry about, but I knew how much he hated dinging one of our cars, let alone two!)

When he talked about taking the cars to the body shop, I said, "I laughed with them the last time and told them, 'We're keeping you in business!'" My response calmed things down. No blame. No drama.

If the blame-and-shame game has been an issue between you and your spouse, try taking a baby step. First, see if you can identify one recurring argument or scenario that often leads you to put blame on your spouse. Then, using some of the suggestions from the bulleted list, make your own plan for how you will respond differently. If it gets messy and doesn't work out as you planned, don't give up. Try again the next time.

tip #2: validate your spouse's emotions

When I worked as a pharmacist, I attended a lecture by a respected palliative-care physician. He talked about his tendency early on in his career to have a very clinical approach as a doctor. He dedicated his life to patients by offering skilled diagnoses and the best treatments available, but he didn't show his emotions while he was treating them. He gradually recognized that he came across as being cold and uncaring, which didn't line up with his values. After all, he was passionate about providing excellent care for his patients.

His advice carried a lasting impact for me:

> By responding and reacting to your patient's emotions, even if you only say a few words, you will come across as being warm and caring. If you skim over them and don't respond, you'll be perceived as cold and indifferent. For example, when your patient goes through the emotional shock of their diagnosis, don't ignore their emotion. Respond to it. Say something like, "It's so difficult to get this news. I feel for you. It's normal to cry . . ."[1]

If a doctor responds and reacts to the patient's emotions instead of ignoring them, he or she forges a closer relationship with the patient.

The same is true in marriage. If you like memory aids, here's one that fits: *Showing your spouse you care builds the bond you share.* In other words, making the effort to read your spouse's emotions and body language and respond to those emotions—validating them—will help build a closer emotional connection between you.

This opens up the vast subject of emotional intelligence. Put into simple terms, emotional intelligence (EI) is the ability to be aware of, manage, and control your emotions and to perceive and respond to the emotions of others with skill and empathy. Just as the doctor learned, by acknowledging and responding to a patient's emotions, he accepted them at face value as legitimate, bringing trust and respect into the relationship. In your marriage, you have a need to be heard and understood emotionally—and so does your spouse. Perhaps your spouse is more melodramatic emotionally and it gets exhausting to empathize with what you perceive as over-the-top emotions. But what if you took a moment to notice his or her emotions and validate them? Don't judge whether the emotions are right or wrong. Don't argue about them either. For example, say, "It seems like you're angry [or whatever the emotion is]. Tell me more." Simply acknowledge your partner's emotions for what they are.

If you find reading your spouse's emotions and accepting them without judgment is a challenge, join the club—for most of us, it is! But it's worth the effort, and fortunately this is a learnable skill. Our emotional intelligence is not static or beyond our control; it isn't an unchangeable part of us, like our height. We can hone our emotional intelligence through practice and reps, just as we build muscle by lifting weights.[2]

That's good news because let's face it—dealing with our kids, pressure at our jobs, our community activities, and our marriages means that we all sometimes find it challenging to respond to our spouses' emotions in ways that feel safe for them.

Carey and I had to learn the hard way how to be emotionally safe for each other. Carey's personality is highly energetic, while I tend to dole out energy like it's a scarce resource. He has the drive to cross even that one last thing off his list, no matter the time. But not me. I feel a sense of dread when faced with something on my to-do list after my physical and emotional reserves are depleted.

Here's an example of our temperaments in conflict. Late one

evening, Carey began to hang window blinds in our bedroom. He needed my help, but I was ready to fall into bed. Our emotions quickly fired up. I felt I didn't have it in me to hang the blinds, even though we'd agreed earlier that we would do it that day. I felt criticized for being tired and drained. Carey felt judged for being frustrated that I had ditched our plan. We lacked insight into how our emotions were mirroring the way we're each wired. We both held that sense of injustice about being judged for how we felt, which only pulled us further apart. We needed to learn how to be emotionally present and safe with each other.

Acclaimed researcher Dr. Sue Johnson teaches couples how to be emotionally present with each other to build a stronger connection. She stresses that couples need to slow down to listen to each other and respond to each other's emotions with compassion and not defensiveness or judgment. This is important to a relationship because our surface conflict may be driven by a basic human need, which is for our loved ones to validate our emotions without criticizing them. When people lash out at each other, it's often because underneath they have hurts related to feeling rejected or they have fears of abandonment. And when a spouse criticizes or judges, those hurts and fears feel more legitimized, and the couple's connection takes a hit. Dr. Johnson leads couples to feel more strongly connected by being open and vulnerable with each other, listening to each other, and responding to the other's emotions. She remarks that by doing so "they have the ability to de-escalate conflicts. But more than that, every time they do this, they are creating a platform of safety on which they can stand to manage the deep emotions that are part of love."[3]

What does an emotionally safe conversation look like? Marriage counselor Dr. Tim Lane uses the following conversations to demonstrate the difference between a *pass* and a *fail* in how one spouse responds to the other's venting at the end of a day.

CASE NUMBER 1

Andy is upset because his life is a roller coaster of workplace politics. When he comes home at the end of the day, he likes to debrief with his wife, Melissa, who is also arriving home from work.

Fail

ANDY: You wouldn't believe what happened today! Jeremy went behind my back and [blocked] a change that I had put in place to increase our department's efficiency. It drives me crazy the way he does this. It feels disrespectful. He reports to *me*.

MELISSA: Well, Andy, you should know by now that he is going to do that. Can't you just confront him? I mean, it is really that simple. I think you should send an email to him saying that you need to talk to him. Don't put it off . . . Let him know who is in charge. If you don't do it now, it will just get worse . . . (blah . . . blah . . . blah).

ANDY: (Dead silence . . .)

Pass

ANDY: You wouldn't believe what happened today! Jeremy went behind my back and [blocked] a change that I had put in place to increase our department's efficiency. It drives me crazy the way he does this. It feels disrespectful. He reports to *me*.

MELISSA: Oh no, this happened again? I am so sorry you had to experience that. . . . You must really be upset.

ANDY: Thank you so much for understanding. Sometimes I just need to share my frustrations, and it helps me to know that you are there for me. I may want to talk with you later tonight once we get the kids to bed. I could use your insight.

CASE NUMBER 2

Sara has been home all day taking care of her five-year-old son and two-year-old daughter. When her husband, Dan, comes home, she shares some of her struggles that she has encountered throughout the day.

Fail

SARA: You wouldn't believe what kind of day I have had. First, Johnny vomited three times from a stomach virus that came out of nowhere. And Jessica has been at it again with her strong-willed nature, pushing all of my buttons. I am exhausted!

DAN: You know, it's so hard to come in the front door every day after I've been at work and listen to you complain about the kids. You need to have a firmer handle on caring for them. I have a job too, but I don't come home complaining about everything that is on my plate . . . (blah . . . blah . . . blah).

SARA: (Silently cries)

Pass

SARA: You wouldn't believe what kind of day I have had. First, Johnny vomited three times from a stomach virus that came out of nowhere. And Jessica has been at it again with her strong-willed nature, pushing all of my buttons. I am exhausted!

DAN: Wow! What a day it has been for you! That's a bummer about Johnny. Is he okay? And I'm sorry you had to deal with Jessica pushing your buttons all day while that was going on. How can I help?

SARA: I am so glad you are home! I know you've had a long day too, but I really could use some help. Thanks![4]

On their own the fails may not appear to be marriage breakers, but the cumulative effects of a person failing to respond in a compassionate way to his or her partner's emotions does wear and tear on their connection. It will push them apart instead of drawing them closer. If you and your spouse are a typical couple, your natural wiring is not the same. You both may react very differently to the same circumstances. So ask yourself, *Am I willing to make space in our relationship for our differences? Can I view my spouse's strengths with admiration and my spouse's weaknesses with compassion?*

Being emotionally present and responsive may not be your natural modus operandi. I grew up in an environment where emotions weren't acknowledged or managed well. But as I said earlier, your emotional intelligence is a skill you can learn. When your partner is emoting, don't jump to be self-defensive or critical. And for sure, don't jump straight into stating the logical thing to do, even if the solution seems dead obvious to you. Try to understand your spouse's emotion from his or her perspective, and show that you care when your spouse is hurting. Once you've acknowledged the emotion and validated it, maybe your next step is simply to ask, "How can I help?"

You may be wondering, *What if my spouse is emoting so much that I'm overwhelmed? There's so much emotion coming at me that I can't handle it anymore!* If you've validated your spouse's emotions, refrained from judgment, and done what you could to help, yet there's still more anger or fear or sadness, then maybe something else is going on. In a calm way, be honest with your spouse about how you feel. Propose that you search together for more insight into where all the emotions are coming from. Encourage your spouse to reach out for help and explain that the emotional weight may be too much for you and your spouse to carry by yourselves. That's fair. A spouse isn't designed to bear the full emotional burden of the other's brokenness. We're meant to be part of a community that's larger than just two people. You know the saying "It takes a village to raise a child"? Well, it applies to marriage too—it takes a village to make a marriage strong. Even if your husband or wife doesn't see the need, don't hesitate to reach out for help from a marriage therapist, psychologist, or medical professional.

tip #3: recognize the need for forgiveness

Forgiveness is far easier to talk about than to carry out. It's such an important part of healing the rifts between you that I've dedicated a whole chapter to it (chapter 8). If you're holding on to resentment, bitterness, or contempt, don't pretend it's not there, for your own sake. Real forgiveness of deep hurts is never easy. Don't expect it to be a onetime effort, once and done.

So why embark on a process of forgiving your spouse that may feel as if you're selling yourself short? Decisions to extend forgiveness, or not, have an impact on our hearts. When you fail to forgive a wrong, you actually create a hard shell around your otherwise soft heart.

With every grievance you hold on to, you make that shell less penetrable. You render the soft heart underneath less available and less open to others. And don't think the shell is selective. You may imagine that holding on to a grievance affects your relationship with the offender only, but it doesn't work that way. The hardness you're creating in your heart doesn't just disappear as you relate to other people. It will still be in the way of you forming real connections. The end condition of a heart encased by an impenetrable shell is isolation. The attention you pay toward forgiving others repays you over time with a heart that is more open to forming richer relationships.

Forgiveness is a process. You can think of forgiveness as water you're releasing onto that hard outer shell. This water eventually forces that hard coating to swell and burst open, just as water makes a seed coat crack to release a miracle seedling. New life emerges through the crack, and the water—forgiveness—made it possible. If you want your relationships with the people close to you (not only your spouse but your friends and kids) to be vibrant and flourish, you can't leave your heart encased in a hard shell.

Lewis Smedes described the forgiveness process using four steps: hurt, hate, heal, come together.[5] While you need to be honest about the facts and the hate you may feel because of the injustice done to you, the process of forgiveness means you actively release—through mercy and humility—the penalty you feel is deserved. In humility you step away from being the judge or the enforcer and search yourself to own your part.

Desmond Tutu also described a fourfold path: tell the story, name the hurt, grant forgiveness, and release or reconcile the relationship. He wrote of a man who released the hatred he'd held for years toward his father, who'd inflicted cruel and inhumane torture on him, his brothers, and his mother. Decades after the unspeakable pain of the man's childhood and after he realized he was carrying his pain into every intimate relationship in his life, he drove his motorcycle up the lane to his elderly father's house. As they both peered into the motorcycle's engine—no words of apology ever having been spoken—the man simply forgave his father. In a moment, his father transformed before his eyes into a human, weak and frail. It was the same moment that this man—who'd been so unconscionably hurt—let go of his anger and bitterness.[6]

Why bother forgiving your partner? Especially when you don't know where your marriage is headed? And there are no guarantees of reciprocity? You forgive so you can live out the miracle of new life, regardless of where your marriage heads. New life grows through the cracks of that hard shell only after you allow forgiveness to do its work.

If you want to try moving closer instead of moving on, you have so many options, and there's no one-size-fits-all. Maybe you need to stop your own rain clouds from dumping blame. Call a time-out when you notice you're heading to the red zone. Refocus your attention on validating your partner's emotions. Perhaps your next step is to get the help you need so that you can do this. Humans are wired to crave love that doesn't have strings attached, and that includes being accepted for who we are—emotions and all. In your conversations with each other, be emotionally present, accept your partner's emotions without judgment, and, whenever possible, ask how you can help. *Showing your spouse you care builds the bond you share.*

FIND WHAT YOU *REALLY* WANT

1. When was the last time you used blame language, such as "You're so self-centered" or "You always . . ." or "You never . . ."? What was your partner's response?
2. When you and your partner air your differences, can you tell the difference between your green, yellow, and red zones? What's your body's primary signal that warns you you're heading into the red zone?
3. Which of the following statements resonates more with you about how you respond to your partner's venting?
   a. "I'm pretty good at accepting my partner's feelings for what they are. I state what I think my partner is feeling so I can be corrected if I've misunderstood."
   b. "I have a tendency to skip over or ignore my partner's emotions and head straight into searching for solutions to the problem my partner is venting about."

   If you answered "b," what steps could you take to get you closer to trying "a"?

CHAPTER 6

stop fighting! how to make peace, starting now

I can't believe you're late again. You promised you wouldn't be!"

"The only person you ever think about is *you*."

"You didn't do what you said you would do—*again*!"

"Do my feelings mean nothing to you?"

You've probably said or heard something like this. Maybe it wasn't that long ago. Maybe your last argument is still ringing in your ears. Your fights with your spouse, along with your anxiety about how your kids are coping, may be a major reason you're thinking about calling it quits.

Splitting is one solution to escape the problem of constant fighting, but is it the best one? Could you instead learn more respectful and effective ways to communicate your disagreements? And if your everyday dealings with each other were easier to digest, would you feel better about your marriage? And closer to your spouse?

It's easy and natural to fight for what you want. You may even sometimes do it without being aware. On the other hand, if you've had negative experiences with conflict, you may try to avoid it. The challenge is that if you want closeness, you can't avoid conflict. Absence of conflict in any long-term relationship is a red flag signaling that someone has disengaged or is overly controlling or is too fearful. Two people leaning in with their own thought processes, ideas, and dreams will lead to differences. If both are engaged, some degree of conflict is inevitable, but it doesn't have to be unhealthy. You can learn the skills of peacemaking to navigate your differences more successfully.

Communication snares, when they are hidden from us, can cause chaos. But it doesn't have to be that way. Of the many couples I've witnessed in conflict, there are some commonalities among their arguments that would be helpful for us to learn from.

Let's shed some light on what may be involved in your conflict. While peacemaking may not come naturally, you can take steps to become more savvy at it, and you may very well get what you deserve—more peace!

are you playing the victim?

I've shared enough of my story to show you how much my relationship with Carey was choked by the ways we carried out conflict. While some of our conflict was aggravated by the things we said, some was driven by the false stories we'd started to believe.

When our kids were young and active and Carey was overwhelmed with his work, he and I often found ourselves at odds. One of the undercurrents of our conflict was how we each chose to use our time. Carey was leading a church that was growing quickly, and he was part of a network of leaders who also wanted the benefit of his many talents. He faced an endless list of requests and demands on his time, and while he was a hands-on dad with our sons, managing time was a challenge.

I was working part-time at a hospital, and as a mom, I had my own endless to-do list. Carey and I clashed over the results of our time pressures, and I struggled with how much I felt disconnected from him. During that season, I often found myself tense, irritable, and brooding. These negative emotions, combined with the seemingly relentless demands for my energy, left me feeling as though all I could do was survive. I'm not saying it was Carey's fault that I was so fatigued, since in reality, various factors were involved.

As I write now about this scenario, I can see straightforward solutions: go back to the basics of schedule management, choose priorities, and focus more on parenting while the kids are young. But the scenario is deceiving, because more was going on than our disconnect over time management. We couldn't have a rational conversation about getting on the same page because we were both telling ourselves a victim story.

I'm guessing you've heard the terms *victim story* and *victim mentality* before. When I believe a victim story or have a victim mentality, I fail to see the whole picture. I begin to manipulate or inflate my spouse's weakness into a story that clouds my vision and encourages me to be passive and avoid responsibility. The thing about a victim story is that while it may contain a kernel of truth, it isn't fully accurate. That kernel of truth gets stretched to a conclusion that goes too far. The conclusion is untrue because it's unidimensional.

For Carey at that stage, his victim story went something like "I have to get all this work done, and because Toni's not doing x, y, and z, it's chaos at home. I'll have to do it all." Meanwhile, my victim story went something like "If Carey wasn't working all the time, I wouldn't feel so overwhelmed, so alone, and too exhausted to get anything done in the evenings." My victim story, which underlaid my thoughts and attitudes, was that I was living the fallout of Carey's workaholism. Carey's victim story was that he was living the consequences of my laziness.

In a victim story, there's reality and then there's fiction—and sometimes they're hard to distinguish. You see, both Carey and I did have a complaint about each other's time management, and our complaints had some grounding in reality. It was true that Carey was overworking, and it was true that I was spending a lot of time in the evenings playing with our kids while other responsibilities were left undone.

Some stories do involve real perpetrators and real victims. Some people are robbed at gunpoint. There really are hit-and-run accidents. And one spouse may actually be defrauded of his savings by the other. But when someone takes a truth about a weakness in her partner and adds her own negative feelings to draw the conclusion that her bad feelings exist because she's being victimized by her spouse's weakness, it's usually an oversimplification. There's some fiction in the story.

What's the fictional part of our victim stories? The fiction both of us believed was our own innocence. I believed that I played no role in the behavior that was at the core of my complaint with Carey. One of the reasons I was alone and exhausted was that I was creating a disincentive for Carey to come home. This disincentive wasn't the lone cause of Carey's overworking, but I did play a role in it. We weren't on the same page in our parenting—I was taking the path of least resistance. It was easier to play with our kids than establish and enforce chore routines for them. For Carey to be home in the evenings and have to work on all the chores that weren't done while the rest of us played (or did homework) made his workplace and its rewards feel more attractive to him. But I couldn't see the fiction in my story, so I blamed him.

On Carey's part, he couldn't see the fiction in his story about what he saw as my "laziness." He wasn't seeing that he, as well, played a role. His habit of working long hours and leaving me alone to handle the home front contributed to my exhaustion. He was taking the path of least resistance and choosing work instead of setting appropriate boundaries between his work life and home life. Maybe I would have had the emotional energy to set and enforce chores for our boys if I'd had more of his support at home during our evenings. As you see, we were both caught in a unidimensional fiction where we secretly each held on to that belief that "I'm a victim of my spouse." But it's not the whole truth.

Anyone who lives with another human will sometimes experience the effect of the other's brokenness. In the vast majority of the marriage fights I've seen, *both* people claim to be the victim in some way, shape, or form. I've never had to ask clients who were fighting with their spouses to justify why their perspectives were better and how they were being victimized. In most cases, clients would lay it out for me early on. Over time, as I witnessed how they interacted during the negotiations and I heard more of the backstory, the unidimensional character of the victim story became abundantly clear.

Here's what embracing a victim story actually does.

YOUR VICTIM STORY CLOUDS YOUR VIEW

Framing a story with yourself as the victim gives it a disproportionate emotional impact in a relationship-distorting way. Once you're a victim, there's a perpetrator. Notice that we don't need to speak this story to ourselves for us to believe it. The underlying belief may be unstated, but it still exists. And in marriage, if you're the victim, then your spouse is naturally the perpetrator. When that happens, you stop appreciating the positive qualities your partner brings to the relationship because you're focusing on how you're a victim of his or her weaknesses.

In my mediation practice, this clouded view was the reason a soon-to-be-divorced person could talk to me one on one and leave me with a mental picture of his or her spouse that proved over time to be a distorted view of who that person was. Typically, not only was the view inaccurate, but it was much less compassionate, more cynical, and, in some cases, crueler than was warranted.

In your conflict, if you've got a victim story underneath your complaint about your spouse—whether it's grounded in reality or fiction—chances are it's clouding your view of who your spouse really is.

YOUR VICTIM STORY MAKES YOU MORE RIGID

If you have a victim story attached to your conflict, you may also be holding your spouse to a more rigid standard than you hold yourself to. Maybe your spouse coming home late from work has been a point of contention between you. As has happened before, she texted you to let you know she'll be home a half hour later than you both agreed to. Your anger is already provoked before she walks in the door. You've already jumped to conclusions: she doesn't know how to set boundaries at work, doesn't know how to say no, or simply cares nothing about your time. And maybe you're thinking, *Now my whole evening is derailed. How can I keep putting up with this?* Well, let's slow down. First, if this is a chronic issue, then it needs real attention. I'm not saying you're being too rigid by reacting to your spouse routinely having a problem with lateness (or overspending or drinking too much, and so on). But let's not confuse a chronic and serious issue with an occasional one; so, let's zero in on how the victim story may influence your responses to your spouse's day-to-day slipups. When you have a scenario like the one above, before you draw any conclusions, try putting the shoe on the other foot.

Imagine *you're* the one who was late. Imagine your partner is the one who's angry before you step through the door. You have a very good explanation. Your boss gave you a last-minute assignment due today. Then on your drive home, you were stuck in traffic because of an accident on the highway. You also had no choice but to stop for gas because, well, you were preoccupied by your presentation on your way to work and didn't notice the tank was almost empty. You view your lateness from the perspective of your intentions and your circumstances.

So with this scenario, if you're looking through a victim mindset, such as "She only thinks about herself" or "He's just a workaholic," you're more likely to draw rigid lines and react with flared emotions when actually the circumstances may call for more flexibility on your part. After all, given the same scenario, you would probably let yourself off the hook.

YOUR VICTIM STORY ENCOURAGES YOU TO BE PASSIVE

When I believe that my spouse's behavior is *the* reason for our conflict or *the* reason for my negative emotions, I can fool myself into being passive. It helps me deny my role in our conflict. Influenced by my victim story, I may abdicate my responsibility to take action. Taking action may not completely solve the conflict or problem, but it's something that is within my control and could very well help our relationship. However, if my tendency in my analysis of our conflict is to look no further than my victim story, I'm always putting myself in the comfortable position. Don't miss this: by choosing the path of least resistance, I was avoiding the difficult step of being more deliberate with my parenting and continued to believe I was the victim of Carey's overworking. My victim story didn't lead me to a better outcome in our marriage or in my parenting, but it made my life easier in the moment—because through my story, I excused myself from taking on the more difficult task. I also used my victim story to leverage attention from the people around me. My friends would commiserate with me while I shared my story. Of course, I didn't refer to it as "my victim story," but that's what it was.

When the victim story is buried inside you and you don't stop to uncover it, it may be driving unhealthy conflict. The partly fictional victim story you're believing may cause resentment or contempt to build inside you, even while it slips under the radar.

A HEALTHY MINDSET BRINGS SELF-AWARENESS

For Carey and me, a lot of our healing began when we took baby steps toward becoming more self-aware by examining ourselves with humility. I can't honestly pinpoint a moment when I had the

Aha! revelation that I viewed myself as a victim. But slowly, as I heeded advice from counselors and friends and dug deeper into my spiritual practices, I began to recognize I'd been clinging to a victim story that was mostly fictional. To make progress, I had to ditch that victim story. Fortunately, both Carey and I were willing to do this. That's when we started to see real change in our conflict levels.

For example, I was struggling with the negative feelings and fatigue I believed arose from being married to a workaholic. I needed some professional help to uncover the root causes for my exhaustion, and they had far more to do with the internal mud I wrote about in chapter 2 than they did with Carey's long hours. My feeling of loneliness had less to do with Carey not being home and more to do with a lie I'd been telling myself. I entered counseling with a clouded view of Carey and—thankfully—began to experience freedom from my distorted perspective. I needed to take responsibility for improving my emotional health and my energy levels, and I needed to stop using my victim story as an excuse.

For a while, our victim stories prevented us from having honest conversations. We both needed to hear from each other about why we felt so burdened regarding the family schedule, but we needed to be heard without each other's distorted views and rigid standards. We needed to listen to each other, free from the perspectives that encouraged us to be passive because it was *his fault* or *her fault*. Ditching our victim stories helped us be more critical of our own behavior, setting our personal bars higher so we could meet each other's desires.

Possibly the most significant peacemaking decision you can make is to stop believing you're a victim, at least the sole victim, in your marriage. You and your spouse are *both* unhappily married. You both have something to contribute to your unhappiness. You are two broken but lovable people trying to make sense of how you ended up *here,* so far from your dream. When you next air your differences with your spouse, say to yourself, *I am not a victim in my marriage.* See if you can uncover what your victim story is, because it may not be obvious at first glance. Then have a conversation with your spouse in which you're curious and listening intently. Take on the challenge to be at least as charitable to your spouse as you are with yourself. Look for the fictional parts to your victim story. Try to uncover your role in the problem and how you can be part of the solution.[1]

what if your spouse isn't always wrong and you aren't always right?

Max and Jenni were struggling through their divorce proceedings. For years as a married couple, they had wrestled with their conflict and had a hard time seeing anything good in each other. Finally, Jenni decided she'd had enough. While Jenni and Max decided to take a reasonable approach to divorce for the sake of their twins and their finances, it became clear in our sessions that this would be a challenge.

Jenni was a talker, while Max said only what he needed to say and not a word more. No matter what the issue was—whether it involved their twins, business, or home—Jenni painted herself as the virtuous one and Max as the villain. Although she spoke politely and used an even tone, her words always flowed in the same direction: she was right and he was wrong. According to her, his character was deeply flawed. Her contempt for him filled the room, but she wasn't the only one displaying contempt. Though Max was much less vocal, his posture made his contempt clear.

In our sessions, Jenni consistently made digs at Max about being the irresponsible, unreliable parent and the spouse who worked too much and spent too much money. However, as I continued to get to know them, I picked up another, nearly opposite, side to that story—in which Max was an engaged dad who had a good relationship with their twins and was working diligently to support their family. But in her anger, Jenni seemed driven to prove him flawed whenever she had the chance.

Jenni didn't see how her "I'm always right and you're always wrong" attitude created an ever-widening chasm. And even though Max remained mostly silent, he held a similar attitude.

The problem was, they didn't address the dynamic earlier in their marriage. Instead, it festered and did its destructive work. From what they individually shared with me, their relationship hadn't always been this way. They both said they had been happy with their married life for the first several years. But this dynamic of "I'm always right and you're always wrong" had taken its toll. Max could have spoken up and told Jenni how he felt about being treated that way, but he didn't. As Max felt more devalued and even powerless at home, he stayed away more. He avoided the situation by working long hours. Even in our meetings, Max's eyes and body went in the opposite direction of where Jenni was seated. He often sat with his head in his hands or with his face shielded, as if physically protecting himself from Jenni's verbal onslaughts.

That was too bad, because both Jenni and Max were bright, attractive, loving, and hardworking parents with good intentions. They had obviously seen something special in each other when they'd started out. Any healthy long-term relationship requires, at a minimum, civility and respect for the other person—something Jenni and Max had lost when they fell into the attitude of "I'm always right."

A great relationship isn't about knowing more than your partner knows, and the goal of marriage isn't to get ahead of your spouse. Believing or acting as if you know more comes from pride and arrogance and doesn't have a place in an authentic partnership. My husband, Carey, points out that you can "right" someone out of your life. Ironically, if you subconsciously engage in a power struggle with your spouse based on "I'm always right," you're way more likely to lose—lose your closeness, your fun, and eventually your relationship.

You may not believe that's your mindset, but ask yourself, *When was the last time I admitted I was wrong?* If you can't remember or if you tied your admission to something wrong that your spouse did or said, then there's a great possibility you're being influenced by this mindset. "I'm always right" will never bring you peace and joy in your marriage.

It's the same with arguments based on "logic." I've heard so many clients say, "She's just not being logical. I've thought through this logically, and so I know . . ." The problem is that the argument based on logic misses the perspective of the other person and the opportunities for people to be creative together. When people play logic as if it's a trump card in their conflict, it doesn't solve anything. This kind of reasoning in a marriage fight usually signals that the person saying it is entrenched, narrow-minded, or controlling.

Applying logic to solve a difference of opinion between two people works only if they agree on their reasoning. And if they followed the same path of reasoning, they wouldn't be in conflict. When the logic argument shows up, it subtly implies there's something faulty about the other person's thought process. The bottom line is that saying your spouse lacks logic when you're arguing is futile. Instead, ask your partner to explain the reasons for his or her value, view, or solution, and listen intently. Open-mindedly. And don't try to think of your response while your partner is talking. Then when it's your turn, walk your partner through your reasoning, explain the *why* of your position, and allow him or her to draw conclusions.

You can break the pattern. Take a step back. Question your assumption that you are right or that you're the logical one. Assume that the right option is *neither* of your opening positions. Determine to search for another resolution you can both agree upon. It will require give-and-take, but the reward is that you will step closer to a happy, healthy marriage.

You may be thinking, *That all sounds well and good, but what do I do if* I'm *the one who's always wrong?* There's no way to sugarcoat this: you're in a challenging position. You'll need to model the way to have more constructive conversations and gently (with your emotions under control) push back on your spouse's attitude. So, when you're facing a difference of opinion, ask the *why* questions so your spouse can explain his or her position. If your partner doesn't reciprocate by asking you to explain your *why,* then raise your opinion—calmly! Be assertive—firm but friendly—about what you need to be satisfied with the outcome. Explain that you're not trying to be controlling or get everything you want but that your opinion needs to be factored into the decision.

Work toward bringing the best out of what you both have to offer. Pride may be at work dividing you. Recognize that underneath the prideful stance of "I'm always right" is a life-limiting fear of being wrong. But the stronger stance is the attitude of humility—the attitude that says, "I can learn something valuable from other people's perspectives, including my spouse's." You have the potential to combine your individual strengths to build a dynamic together that is stronger than your influence would be if you were alone.

fight for "we" instead of "me"

When you're in a season of conflict, you may feel criticized or under attack. You may feel the need to protect yourself. That's natural but counterproductive if what you really want is to save your marriage. What if you started to see yourself not as the defender of "me" but as the defender of "we"?

Emily and Kyle had been married eighteen years, and their children were almost adults. During their separation proceedings, Kyle's controlling nature became more evident. All appointments were scheduled for his convenience, regardless of Emily's commitments. As they were sorting out their individual contributions to joint expenses, Kyle made sure the money owed between them was exact to the penny, even though they had ample savings.

Throughout their marriage, Kyle assumed control over their finances, meticulously maintaining records and telling Emily what she could spend, even though she worked as a nurse full time and earned a salary equivalent to his. He had to have the final say in every disagreement. Any input from Emily regarding decisions of any kind was ignored. "What does she know?" was Kyle's evident attitude.

After a while, Emily was so bothered by the power imbalance that she tried to coax Kyle into marriage counseling. Kyle dismissed the need. *What could be wrong with me?* he reasoned. For years, Emily was sufficiently distracted by her work and raising their kids to justify staying in their marriage.

After a couple decades of trying to stretch for a more balanced, mutual relationship, Emily gave up. She decided she couldn't live any longer in a relationship in which she had no say. Kyle wanted to stay married, but over *that* decision he had no control.

Dealing with how power is shared in a marriage is critical. According to Dr. John Gottman, it is the man in the marriage who more often feels threatened by his wife's influence, because at a deep level he resists loss of power. But Dr. Gottman's research shows there's an 81 percent chance a marriage will implode if a man refuses to share power with or be influenced by his wife.[2] What does this mean? At the most fundamental level, it means that neither spouse can have the attitude that he or she holds a veto over what the other spouse thinks, believes, or decides. It also means that a spouse cannot make major life decisions without his or her spouse's input and buy-in. If you want your marriage to be all it can be, you need to view it not as a relationship you control but as a partnership—the fabric of which is made from weaving together negotiations, compromises, and jointly made decisions. If you reach an impasse over a decision, it simply means you'll need to be creative and find another process that helps you both move past it together. It may be that one of you will take on the role of the primary decision maker for certain areas, such as home decor or vacation planning or the family budget, but that's a choice that you've made together, not the result of one of you assuming control through manipulating or shutting down input from the other. There's a difference.

You may have heard or been influenced by the cultural or faith-based belief that the man is the head of the family. Carey and I dealt with this in our marriage too. This belief, separated from its authentic origins that go beyond the scope of this book, can sound sexist, ridiculous, and even misogynistic. However, where it is practiced within the boundaries of loving leadership that seeks only to benefit others, the result within the marriage and family can be beautiful. But when the head-of-the-family concept isn't practiced that way, it becomes complicated or even harmful. Practically speaking—and Dr. Gottman's research supports this—we're more likely to achieve healthier outcomes when we view ourselves as a team. A team that is mutually loving, mutually vulnerable, and mutually self-giving. Carey and I have discovered that committing to listening to each other, searching for shared values and solutions we can both live with, and paying attention to and accommodating our different conflict-resolution styles makes us both better peacemakers. The "we" approach moves us away from unproductive and sometimes destructive debates over whether one person is the head of the marriage.

So, let's shift back to the practical. What does sharing power with your spouse look like in your everyday life? Spoiler alert: the example that follows may look messy, and I say that's okay. Though the decision-making process may take longer and not be as black-and-white, sharing power builds stronger bonds relationally.

Carey and I needed an area rug for our living room. I had dreamt up the perfect rug in my head already—we just had to find it. Carey brought home one that was a checkerboard pattern of cream, burgundy, and periwinkle-blue squares. It was okay, but the rug I had in my mind had less burgundy, though the hues were similar, and a more whimsical, artsy vibe to it—not squares. I was confident I could do better, so we carted that one back to the carpet store. Settling for less than awesome wasn't an option. So, the search continued.

CAREY: How about this one?

TONI: Um, too boring.

CAREY: I like this. It has a bit of blue in it.

TONI: Hmm . . . no, not the right texture.

CAREY: Here's one that's really cool.

TONI: No.

CAREY: Come on, let's just make a decision. Let's buy this one.

TONI: It's not really what I had in mind.

On and on we went. From rug shops to carpet warehouses and even to a neighboring city for more selection. Surely we'd find the carpet that matched my vision—or one even better. We inspected what seemed like thousands of carpets. As we walked out one store after another, Carey kept saying, "Let's just go back and get that first checkerboard carpet and be done with it." He insisted the carpet in my mind didn't exist!

Turns out, he was right. I couldn't find it.

The next evening, I went back to the first store and surveyed the checkerboard of cream, burgundy, and periwinkle-blue squares with the "I told you so" bubble drifting above it. It wasn't the carpet of my dreams, for sure. But I decided to live with it. Carey liked it, it completed our living room, and it was good enough.

We've had way too much conflict and hard feelings over decor decisions. During our early decor disputes, we were overly emotional, overly opinionated, and overly critical of each other. At the beginning, we were both trying to persuade the other to adopt our own personal taste. When we did this, we were fighting for our own turf, like mini warlords claiming the top of two separate hills, ignoring the chasm in between. It's a doomed strategy from the start.

Carey and I needed to learn to value a process that strengthened our relationship more highly than we valued satisfying our individual desires. We changed our attitudes and became willing to compromise some of our wants for the sake of our connection with each other. Over time, we learned that our decor tastes overlap by about 5 to 10 percent. So we now know from experience to be patient and open-minded until we find a design we can both live with. It's about fighting for "we" over fighting for "me"—fighting for unity rather than fierce independence.

Our shared priority is that both of us will be satisfied with the outcome when we have our differences. To fight for "we" instead of fighting for "me," we need to pay attention to the views and tastes of the other. We discovered that working to persuade one spouse to adopt the other spouse's point of view was pushing us apart instead of drawing us closer. We'd both tried and failed at "fighting dirty"—using subtly belittling or critical put-downs to get the other to surrender. If I know Carey will be unhappy with a particular choice, then I don't push for it. Carey does the same for me. Both of us refuse to consider a choice that leaves the other person unsatisfied.

If you find yourself fighting for "me," what if you shifted your focus? What if you could see your differences of opinion as an opportunity to discover each other more deeply and embrace the challenge of being tolerant of, even celebrating, your differences? A lot of issues couples argue over aren't high stakes, and the potential resolutions aren't binary. If you are open to really listening to what your partner is saying and leaning into your collective creativity, you'll start to realize you have way more than two potential solutions.

For example, in Kyle and Emily's case, what if Kyle had asked Emily, "What changes would you make to our budget?" Even if Kyle didn't feel like asking the question, what if he asked it anyway? And what if he wasn't defensive when he heard her answer? Let's say Emily is mostly on board with the budget but wants to save up for a weekend getaway for the two of them to that out-of-town art museum. Maybe Kyle has never had any time for the arts, but what if he went along with the plan to make Emily's dream come true, while keeping a good attitude? What if he made the decision to fight for "we" by listening to Emily? Fast-forward to the end of their trip. Turns out, it was a great weekend. While Kyle may have discovered he isn't all that interested in paintings, he found something fascinating about the art of sculpting. Kyle's decision to be flexible and give Emily some say helped him realize there may be aspects of his own wiring that he's been closed to in the past. There is a part of him that appreciates art, and this new-found appreciation helps him realize he may have a creative side. And he finds this new thought energizing. And Emily? Well, she couldn't stop talking about the thrill of her discoveries at the museum, but more importantly, she was surprised and delighted that Kyle showed an interest in her dream. His care made her want to reciprocate.

Just give it a try. Be open-minded.

Carey and I do have conflict, even now that our marriage is thriving. But in our disagreements now, we prioritize the fight *for* each other's hearts and our marriage above whatever personal stake we have in the issue at hand. To do this, we start from a platform of safety. We view each other as teammates, not opponents. While this is difficult to do when you are stuck in a vicious cycle and feel ambivalent about your marriage, it's a vital part of fighting for your relationship. It's all too easy to slip into a mindset that deceives you into believing that your spouse is your opponent or even the enemy. See if you can say this to each other out loud: "You are worth fighting for!" Don't even worry if it sounds awkward or feels silly. Just say it. And whenever you need a reminder, say it again.

Let's imagine you're creating the family budget and you have a difference of opinion about whether the last three hundred dollars need to be allocated to your long-term savings or your fund for a trip to that tropical resort. Do you split the difference and allocate half to each? Do you save for the vacation and then shift your priority to long-term savings afterward? Do you save for a less expensive vacation? Do you develop an additional income stream? The point is that in a spirit that values your togetherness, you weigh the potential outcomes. You both work on making the adjustments in your relationship so that when you're making these decisions, you can stand side by side, arm in arm, looking in the same direction. The point of this is not to get the best possible outcome for every decision you make together; the point is to have an attitude that focuses on fighting for the strongest version of "we."

Embrace new ways of handling your differences and becoming true partners, and you too may look back on your marriage and be grateful for your hard-fought peace.

FIND WHAT YOU *REALLY* WANT

1. What is similar and what is different about your conflict-resolution style and your partner's? What do you know about each other's personality differences?
2. Can you spot a fictional angle to a victim story you've been telling yourself? If so, how have you been following a path of least resistance but not seen it because of your victim-story narrative?
3. What would you need to change personally to more consistently solve problems with your spouse as a team—to fight for "we" instead of fighting for "me"?

CHAPTER 7

your conflict affects your kids more than you realize

I had to leave. Things are so bad between us, and our kids have seen too much already."

"Our fighting is too toxic. We need to split for the sake of our kids."

"It's terrible being under one roof. It's like a cold war. I just can't do this anymore."

As a divorce attorney, I routinely heard parents make statements like these. Sure, some were more optimistic and said, "We've been separated, but we're amicable and our kids are adjusting." But even most of those who started off as amicable found themselves arguing over parenting decisions after they split. Although many left their marriages at least in part because of their fighting, they discovered it didn't stop after they had separated. In some cases, the fighting escalated.

It's common for children to witness dysfunctional conflict between their parents at home. We all know this experience isn't limited to kids whose parents are divorcing. Unhealthy conflict occurs between spouses before divorce and between couples who stay together. The truth is, our kids join us on the journey through the rough seasons in our marriages. When we parents are in a season of discord, it's easy for us to make the mistake of leaning emotionally on our kids. But looking for emotional comfort or validation or support from our kids only draws them into the mess.

Those mistakes are problematic because your child needs *both* of you. From that starting point, I want you to see how you can help your children be emotionally healthy while you and your spouse work through your challenges. Before I do, though, I'll give you a window into what can happen when parents lose their focus.

the problem with deferring peace

Judge Alex Pazaratz in Hamilton, Ontario, had witnessed the consequences of parents fighting after separating, so he wrote a very succinct and insightful warning to divorcing parents:

> *Breaking Bad,* meet *Breaking Bad Parents.*
>
> The former is an acclaimed fictional TV show whose title needed a bit of explaining: "*BREAKING BAD:* A southern U.S. expression for when a good person suddenly loses their moral compass and starts doing bad things."
>
> The latter is a sad reality show playing out in family courts across the country. "*BREAKING BAD PARENTS:* When smart, loving, caring, sensible mothers and fathers suddenly lose their parental judgment and embark on relentless, nasty litigation; oblivious to the impact on their children."
>
> SPOILER ALERT: The main characters in both of these tragedies end up pretty much the same: Miserable. Financially ruined. And worst of all, hurting the children they claimed they were protecting. . . .
>
> Will these parents sign up for the permanent cast of *Breaking Bad Parents*? Will they become regulars in our fam-

ily court building, recognizable by face and disposition? Or will they come to their senses; salvage their lives, dignity (and finances); and give their children the truly priceless gifts of maturity and permission to love? . . .

I hope I didn't offend the parties with my *Breaking Bad Parents* analogy. They're not bad parents. *Yet.* Mainly, I was trying to give both parties a sobering warning: Stop!

Stop being nasty.

Stop jockeying for position.

Stop playing hardball.

Stop acting like you hate your ex more than you love your children.[1]

A case like the one Judge Pazaratz described is not far-fetched. For some families, it is all too real. But not every case that merits a warning to parents is as easy to spot. Take, for example, Katie and Mac's divorce. They separated when their two boys were seven and four. Mac called it quits because he couldn't stand the constant tension with Katie anymore. After Mac moved out, Katie didn't mean to let it slip in front of their boys how frustrated she was that Mac didn't pay child support on time. She didn't think about the emotional impact on the boys when she vented about her expenses piling up. Mac didn't intend to complain to his kids that their mother didn't care if he had no money left to spend on them. And Mac didn't mean anything by telling his younger son not to tell Mom that Dad forgot the car seat. He just wanted to spend time with his sons without friction from Katie. Then there was the time the boys returned to Katie with sunburns because their dad forgot the sunscreen, which was followed by Katie venting about how irresponsible he was and how much he acted like a child and . . . You get the picture.

Throughout the separation proceedings, I would hear Mac and Katie both say they didn't want their kids caught in the middle.

But in the heat of the moment, the words just leaked out and they couldn't stop venting about the other parent, even when their boys were around.

They weren't bad people or unloving parents—very much the opposite. But their unresolved issues, their mutual resentment, and the lack of trust between them poisoned their dealings and left an impact on their boys. What both Katie and Mac really wanted was the best for their kids. Their children needed to feel loved and free to love both parents, yet they couldn't experience that freedom while their parents openly expressed disdain for each other.

Maybe you believe the bad blood between you and your spouse and its impact on your children is the reason to separate. Let's analyze this idea. Your children have already been exposed to your fighting, and, yes, it may be taking an emotional toll. They may need some help to deal with what they've already seen and heard. But splitting from your spouse is not a quick fix for your children. You can quit your marriage, but you won't quit being co-parents. If you split now because of your fighting, you and your spouse will still have your trigger points and emotionally loaded pasts to deal with. Your unresolved issues with your spouse will not disappear when you walk out the door, and your separation will give you even more unresolved problems. If you split to get rid of the fighting or tension, you still will not get rid of your need to improve the ways you communicate with each other as co-parents. Splitting may reduce the overall time you spend in conflict. Or it may not. Splitting may make it easier to deny—temporarily—that the two of you have communication problems or unresolved issues.

If you want the best for your kids post-divorce, you most likely can't be "done" with your ex. The issues you've left unresolved will continue to trip you up and burden your children. Your kids will be far better off if you both find a way to cooperate.

In my law practice, I persistently encouraged my clients who were parents to seek professional help to work on their dysfunctional communication habits for the sake of their kids. I could see my clients needed assistance to work through their bitterness, resentment, and contempt and move toward each other so they could have civil, sensible conversations about parenting decisions. Many resisted. Why? Though I'm sure other factors were part of their reasoning, they didn't want to invest time, effort, and money into a painful relationship they'd decided to leave behind.

The parents who took me up on my advice usually made that decision once they faced an impasse. They realized their loaded pasts were preventing them from making necessary decisions, such as what parenting schedule would be best or how much money should be paid for child support—or other complex parenting decisions, such as which community to relocate the children to, how to arrange childcare for a child with special needs, or what kind of treatment to choose for a serious illness. Raising kids while apart became too messy and too complicated for them to handle without experienced help, so they chose counseling rather than going straight to court. Though it didn't obviate the court process in all cases, having both parents really engaged helped them raise their kids in an environment that was more peaceful and emotionally secure.

What if you focus on achieving peace and better cooperation between you and your spouse before you make a final decision about splitting? What if you park divorce, and all the logistics that go along with it, long enough to allow you to work on better shielding your kids from your unhealthy conflict now? Perhaps set the marriage decision to the side and learn a few new skills or strategies to help you manage the conflict between you as parents. Chances are, you have the option to defer your decision over whether to split or to save your marriage. Unless moving out is urgent—say, your relationship is harmful versus unhappy—you could both focus your immediate attention on how to support your children during this rough season. You could work on treating each other as having value and being worthy of respect because you are both beloved by your children.

How do you do that? By following three basic guidelines. These are based on some major pitfalls I observed in families going through divorce, but you and I may also see these pitfalls arise between any parents, regardless of marital status.

By basic, I do not mean simple. I use the word *basic* here in the sense of being fundamental to your child's emotional well-being. If you've been struggling to reconcile your differences for years, please don't hear me say that reorienting your relationship as parents will be easy or simple—far from it. You may have to brace yourself for serious internal resistance while you work on these basics.

Whether you eventually split, survive, or save your marriage, if you both can get these three basics right, your kids will benefit more than you know, now and in their future.

basic guideline #1: be kind and respectful

"We need a bonfire pit. All of my friends have one!" said our son who had been lobbying for a firepit for a while. Finally one Saturday, Carey and our sons gathered some decent-sized stones and dug a circular patch out of the sod at the back of our yard. When we were ready for the inaugural fire, our boys were so excited, they couldn't even wait till nightfall. We were planning to roast hot dogs for dinner under the sun and sit around the embers, watching the stars come out.

As they piled up the kindling and logs just so, I stayed busy in the kitchen, cutting the hot dogs so they would roast into "spiders" and getting the condiments ready. Next thing I heard was frantic shouting—"Get the hose!" (Carey yelled this in a panic, mainly to himself since there was no other grown-up in closer proximity to the hose.) I looked out the kitchen window to see

Carey running with all his strength from flames leaping twelve feet in the air. As I rushed outside, Carey ran back with the garden hose and began taming the massive flames. Once there was no more threat from the fire, I turned to see if the kids were okay. They looked pale and shocked. Soon the whole story came out: deciding to give the bonfire a boost, Carey had grabbed the leftover gas from the snowblower sitting in the garage.

My words spewed out faster than water from the hose. "How could you let this happen? With the kids right here! What were you *thinking*?" It's true I was afraid to think of what could have happened, but that was no excuse for letting our kids hear me talk down to their dad. Carey wasn't expecting the mushroom cloud of flames that had erupted, and he was mortified by the whole incident. He had made a simple mistake. But I was disrespectful to him, and that's a problem.

Acting in ways that are generally respectful and kind isn't a problem for all divorcing couples. I witnessed some couples display a decent amount of cooperation and compassion for each other after they separated. They didn't struggle with their tone toward each other. They could resist making personal jabs. Yet I found these parents were a clear minority.

Even in the case of the fire, where you might say we had a legitimate safety concern to talk about, my choice of words and timing were ignorant of respect and kindness. If I could do it again, immediately after the flames were tamed, I would have asked the kids how they were feeling, and I would have talked about how grateful I was that no one was seriously burned. Then later, out of earshot of the kids, I would have calmly and without judgment asked for Carey's take on what had happened. We could have decided together how to debrief the kids about the incident. After all, there was no urgency. They'd already learned firsthand a larger-than-life lesson about gasoline and fire safety. Debriefing in the heat of the moment while everyone's emotions were triggered wasn't a helpful strategy.

When our emotions are triggered by a fight-or-flight reaction, we may seriously struggle in our attempts to shield our kids from the dysfunctional ways we carry out our conflict. One parent may view the discord as being driven by the other parent and feel innocent and helpless to do anything about what the children are seeing and hearing. Some parents may be able to see clearly how the ongoing rift between them is showing up in their children's behavior. But some get distracted by the rift: they focus on their children's behavior as evidence of just how ignorant, stubborn, and difficult the *other parent* is rather than trying to reduce the rift for the children's sake. A parent's mindset of "It's all my spouse's fault" reduces a complex relational dynamic to one that's unidimensional. To which I say, "Come on. Let's be real." If you're fighting in front of your kids, *both* of you are part of the problem and *both* of you need to be part of the solution. Are you willing to own your part?

Developing more kindness and respect between you requires you to find ways to exchange your views. You need to hear what your partner has to say (whether you think so or not!). Your partner needs to hear what you have to say. Typically, this involves having a quiet and undisturbed adult conversation away from your kids. For some couples, even listening to each other is a challenge. It's common for one of you to talk and one of you to withdraw when you have differences of opinion. You may have heard it described as the skunk and the turtle. The skunk spews spray all over everything, everywhere, and the turtle withdraws into its shell.

You both have thoughts that are worth considering, and somehow you'll need to communicate your views on hot-button issues, even if one of you tends to be less talkative. Maybe a simple conversation will work for both of you, but that may not be the only effective way. Maybe one of you needs to write your thoughts in a letter. Or you may need a counselor or a mediator to help you get through a particularly difficult conversation.

Do you believe your spouse has *anything* valuable to say about your parenting decisions? If your answer is yes—even if it's a be-grudging yes—then woo-hoo! Focus on listening to each other and searching for solutions that satisfy you both. If your answer is no, then I suggest you do some soul-searching. What has led you to discount your partner's role as a parent?

If your kids have been witnessing disrespect and unkindness between you as parents, hold a family meeting. Make this a kickoff to a new era in your family life, where kindness and respect are valued. Your kids already know there's a problem. They probably have been exposed more than you think. Even when your kids are in bed, they hear more than you might realize. So, the most heal-ing thing you can do is be real with them and talk about what's been happening. Though your kids don't need a rundown of your issues. Don't let them in on the financial details or the problems with in-laws or the other adult challenges complicating your con-flict.

The crux of the issue is this: If you don't display respect for their other parent, what kind of message does that send your kids about *their* respect for that parent? What kind of message does it ultimately send your kids about *you*? Remember that you as a par-ent are modeling attitudes and behaviors—hopefully ones you wish your children will adopt.

Simply apologize for the disrespectful or unkind ways you've been treating their other parent. It may sound like "I'm sorry I spoke that way to your mom. I sounded mean, and I shouldn't have been. That's not what I intended. Your mom deserves your re-spect, and I respect her too." Or "I complained to you about your dad not listening to me, and I shouldn't have done that. We're working on communicating better with each other, but you don't need to worry about that. You have a great dad who deserves your respect, and I respect him too."

Sometimes parents worry about losing their authority with

their kids by admitting they did or said something wrong, but if you've been unkind to each other in front of your kids, they know it. If the words or actions were hurtful, your kids feel the pain too. The most healing thing you can do is name whatever was hurtful in what you did or said and reinforce your children's sense of right and wrong by owning up to it and apologizing. They will love and respect you more for your humility and honesty, not less.[2] Working to cultivate an atmosphere of respect for each other's views and kindness in the ways you relate to each other in front of your kids will go a long way toward creating a safe emotional space for them at home.

basic guideline #2: value your children's relationship with their other parent

Let's look at what happened with Joel and Esther during their trial separation. Their six-year-old son, Tyson, continued living with Esther and her parents. The conflict between Joel and Esther wasn't relieved by them living in separate homes, because they were arguing more than ever over parenting decisions and Tyson's schedule. Esther wasn't paying attention to how much she vented about Joel while Tyson was around. Esther's frequent vocal complaints about Joel eventually affected Tyson. He started acting up whenever he was with Joel. Tyson's acting out started escalating into regular episodes of defiant outbursts whenever he and Joel were out in public.

Esther decided to seek counseling for herself and Tyson. Though Joel wasn't completely on board with counseling, he didn't outright oppose it.

Through counseling, Esther learned to keep her personal opinions and conflict with Joel private from Tyson. Even though she was still frustrated and angry with Joel, she started to say only positive things about him while Tyson was around. She asked her parents to do the same. She didn't complain to her friends on the phone when Tyson was in the house. She also learned to support Joel's decisions when Tyson was staying with him, even though Joel's parenting style was different from her own. After all, when pressed by her counselor, she had to admit that Joel's decisions weren't dangerous or irresponsible; they just didn't line up with what she would have decided.

Tyson trusted his counselor with his thoughts about his parents separating, and he started a picture journal to express his feelings. Even though Joel didn't completely agree with the counseling plan at the beginning, he did notice its benefits when Tyson's defiant episodes became less intense and less frequent. Tyson's interest in his schoolwork picked up, and Joel started to spend more time helping Tyson with his homework. Although it wasn't easy for either of them, Joel and Esther were able to stop competing over time and parenting strategies, stopping the cycle of resentment and blame they had been caught up in. They eventually made excellent progress in becoming civil with each other for Tyson's sake.

Even if you aren't in a trial separation as Joel and Esther were, if your fighting causes an impact on your parenting, your kids may get the message that you don't approve of their affection for their other parent. Your body language and your facial expressions toward your partner may be communicating more than you think. If you're experiencing serious tension in your marriage, you may be leaning on your children emotionally. Maybe you're confiding in them about how the other parent is making your life harder. Maybe you're looking to be consoled by someone and you turn to your kids for comfort. You may be looking for your kids' approval. In the process of doing these things, you're burdening them with adult issues and undermining their bond with their other parent. Without ever intending to do it, you may be saddling your kids with worries and fears about their personal security and attitudes of disdain toward their other parent. You may be drawing them out of their childhood into an adult world.

Even though Esther was unknowingly contributing to Tyson's outbursts, she did something well—she valued Tyson's relationship with Joel. She didn't use Tyson's outbursts as evidence that Tyson should have less contact with Joel. And she didn't blame the outbursts on Joel's inability to parent. Though initially she didn't recognize the impact her venting had on Tyson's behavior, once she did realize it, she made some changes. Joel, to his credit, didn't oppose the counseling that proved to help Tyson. To Joel's surprise, it helped strengthen his bond with Tyson.

By supporting Tyson's relationship with Joel and getting Tyson into counseling, Esther guarded Tyson's heart. Every child inherently knows that he or she is part of both parents. If you tear down your child's other parent, you also tear down a part of your child's sense of worth. Valuing your children's relationship with their other parent may mean you have to do some things that feel difficult, like keeping quiet and journaling instead of venting, calling and confiding in a friend privately instead of talking to your kids about it, and agreeing to counseling even though you've believed in the past it was for people who are weak or soft but not for people who have it together.

Whatever you do, don't place your kids in the heartbreaking position of having to take sides by asking them to choose between you and your spouse. Younger kids will tell each of you what they think you want to hear, and they may tell each of you opposite things because they're wired to avoid the risk of losing their bond with either of you. Asking kids to take sides asks them to devalue their other parent and places them right in the middle of your fighting.

Research shows that children fare best when they have relationships—with both parents—that are as healthy as they can be under the circumstances.[3] See if you can put yourself in your children's shoes and place the utmost value on their other parent.

basic guideline #3: co-parent from a posture of unity

When showing kindness and respect to each other is a challenge, trying to make parenting decisions together may only add fuel to the fire. Yet it's essential to present a united parenting front.

If you've been parenting for any length of time, you've already realized that you and your spouse have different ideas about how to raise kids. Behavior that is acceptable to one of you isn't to the other. For example, one of you may be more lenient about bedtimes and routines. Or one of you may allow for rougher play. Or one of you may have more of an aversion to the children making noise and messes. But there's quite a bit of latitude in what you can consider acceptable or reasonable—aside from making sure your kids are reasonably protected from harm.

Often if one parent is anxious while the other is not, the anxious parent will tend to discount the behavior of the non-anxious parent as careless or inattentive.[4] However, the non-anxious parent has something to offer the child too by counterbalancing the impact of that parent's anxiety. Author and counselor Sissy Goff says to the anxious parent, "Both of your voices are important, and his or her lack of anxiety helps to even out the effect of your anxiety."[5] Kids also benefit from taking risks, being encouraged to do something they can *almost* do, and facing the scary thing.

So, to co-parent from a posture of unity, you make the effort to reach a consensus with your spouse on your overall parenting goals. You work together to establish consistent values. These values may be big picture, such as "We want our children to have loving relationships with both their parents" or "We want our children to feel loved and accepted by their larger family on both sides" or "We want our children to value good nutrition, physical activity, and plenty of sleep" or "We want our children to value education." The overall goals may still require negotiating, but you can move the focus away from the specifics of parenting styles. Chances are, your styles are not going to be the same, so don't start there. If you were carbon copies of each other, your children would have a shallower pool of wisdom, skills, street smarts, and life experience to learn from. But you aren't, so your kids stand to benefit more if they have strong and healthy bonds with each of you.

How do you work toward a posture of unity while you're struggling with conflict? I worked with many clients who were distressed over this problem. Take Chelsea and Josh, for example. They separated after nine years of marriage and struggled to parent their son and daughter, ages seven and four. Chelsea was raised in a large city and preferred urban living, while Josh spent most of his time working remotely from the lake home they'd built north of the city. Josh liked to take the kids canoeing, skiing, and wilderness camping, but Chelsea tended toward a more protective parenting approach and was always stressed about whether Josh was being attentive enough to their kids' safety when they were staying with him. In the early days of their separation, she was adamantly opposed to him having the kids overnight.

Chelsea and Josh decided to work with a mediator to develop a parenting plan, with the goal of reducing their fighting over parenting decisions. They reasoned that if they worked out some of those parenting decisions in advance, they would have less to argue over. They took several sessions over an eight-week period and managed to reach an agreement on many issues surrounding school, extracurricular activities, vaccination schedules, religious instruction, and vacations. They acknowledged that they might return to mediation for help in creating a plan for their children's teenage years: balancing work or sports with studies, creating and enforcing curfew, and planning for their post-secondary education.

After a year with their mediated parenting plan in place, Chelsea and Josh were spending less time and energy arguing with each other and more time enjoying their kids.

If you aren't on the same page with your parenting decisions and can't find your way to a compromise, seek out a family mediator or trained therapist and work on a parenting plan. Or agree to have your children see an expert you both approve of and follow his or her advice. It's okay to agree to disagree with each other, but you still need to find the right process that will help you both make parenting decisions and keep the peace between you for the sake of your children.

When your spouse makes a parenting decision on everyday issues, such as when homework should be done and whether or not the kids can have a sleepover, support it. If you need to air your differences about the decision, do it privately, away from your kids. Avoid undermining each other's decisions in front of your kids. Work to get on the same page so you can be as consistent as possible.

Your goal in all this is to offer your kids stability and security and to give them the benefit of appropriate boundaries. Parenting from a posture of unity means you're both focused on loving your kids and raising them according to a wise plan without being distracted by your adult-relationship woes that may take longer than your kids' childhood years to fully resolve.

the time for more peace is now

Being in the middle of a season of conflict feels chaotic, so the last thing I want for you is more chaos. Changing behavior isn't easy, but I don't want your next step to be complicated. I'm asking you to pick one single next step. That's it. One. Maybe this one step will be to call a family meeting and make one apology. Or make a point to say one positive thing about your spouse in front of your children today. Or perhaps, when your spouse makes an inconsequential parenting decision that you don't agree with, hold your tongue in the moment rather than tearing down your spouse in front of your kids. Once you've done that one step, you're free to choose the next one.

There's no time to waste if your kids are being affected by the bad blood between you. This is urgent business for you to handle. If you've seen the family law world yourself or if your own parents have gone through a divorce, maybe you feel this urgency too.

A wise, experienced divorce attorney once pleaded with me and some of my colleagues to take seriously the children's suffering in messy separations. He appealed to us, a group of family lawyers, to make achieving peace for the sake of the kids a top priority. He had witnessed too many parents fighting to win the war they were all caught up in. He felt the urgent need to stop kids from being in the cross fire. When parents are pitted against each other, the toll it takes on kids' emotional and mental health is more serious than we realize.

The imagery the attorney used was shocking: when kids are exposed to ongoing, unmitigated conflict between their parents, something inside them dies. When kids are caught in the middle of toxic conflict between their parents, we might as well see the kids floating facedown in a pool—drowning. When parents are warring, kids are drowning in strife. Horrific? Yes, but not overstated.

If there's a real spirit of competitiveness, aggression, contempt, or malice between you and your spouse, the time for peace is *now*. You need to do something about it. I'm not saying this in judgment. I'm not trying to be dramatic. But I think the lawyer's compelling point—along with his imagery, as abhorrent as it is—stands to help us.

If you are parenting while you're engaged in unhealthy conflict, you have a challenge on your hands. You have a choice. Your words and actions can lead to a little more life or a lot more suffering for your kids.

I know what you *really* want is to choose a little more life.

FIND WHAT YOU *REALLY* WANT

1. Does the way you treat your spouse in front of your family typically come off as respectful or disrespectful? What behavior do you notice in your children that mirrors your approach and attitude toward your spouse?
2. If a fly on the wall in your home over the past week could talk, what kind of story would it tell about the emotional security of your children's environment?
3. Do you ever talk to your children about their other parent's strengths? How do you respond when your children, unsolicited, bring up their other parent's weaknesses?

CHAPTER 8

where could steps of forgiveness take you?

It was our lowest moment. We'd had hints of discord before we left the driveway. Carey and I had struggled through a hectic week during another hurried season, and neither of us possessed the patience or lightheartedness that might avert a war born of pent-up frustrations. Irritability escalated to bickering and then to a full-out argument. Our original plan for a date night was simple: grab a latte and take a moonlit waterfront walk. We followed the plan despite our darkened moods until, coffees in hand, we sat in the front seats of our car in the café parking lot—screaming at each other. And with a sweeping thrust of my arm, I pitched the coffee at Carey and threw away our attempt at intimacy. In my mind, we were finished.

As we headed home, we no longer yelled. We spoke in measured and dispassionate tones. But the topic was clear: we were seriously contemplating our lives apart from each other. We considered where each of us might live and what it might feel like to say goodbye to our kids for days at a time. Neither of us wanted to face that pain, nor did we want to turn our minds to the consequences this would have on our ministry.

It was likely no coincidence that our route home took us past the country road that led to our church building. We both felt drawn to carry on this critical conversation within the walls of the church we were pouring our lives into. In our crisis of chaos and desperation, we dragged ourselves to the front of the auditorium and sat on the steps leading up to the platform. As we surveyed the empty seats—seats that every week held souls searching for love and hope—I wondered if we would ever find enough love and hope to purge the contempt we both felt and to mend our shredded bond. As we spoke about parting, the weight of our alternate reality held us still. Our relationship had become terrible, yes. Yet what we saw with our eyes reminded us that hate couldn't have the final word. We needed to somehow break free from hurt and bitterness and resentment. Sitting on those steps, we both knew the only thing that would truly do that: forgiveness.

building steps of forgiveness

When I think of how much I needed to confess my own shortcomings and ask Carey for forgiveness and how much we needed to wrestle with granting forgiveness, I remember that critical night on those steps. We knew we couldn't sit there forever. Because steps aren't constructed for passivity; they're made for action. They're built to take people somewhere, from here to there, one story to another, up or down.

It makes me think of another kind of steps: aged stone steps, well worn, traveled by countless feet over thousands of years, that lead to a castle that stands today to testify of centuries gone by. When tourists visit these ancient sites, the steps don't get the attention. Only the castle or the cathedral does. But we don't reach the historic site without walking over the steps.

How do those steps remain intact? Three essential ingredients combine to create sturdy steps: stone, mortar, and water. Without these three ingredients, the final product isn't permanent. Stones on their own will shift. Mortar by itself will break down. And water evaporates. But combine all three, and the structure designed to take people places will endure generation after generation.

Picture these stone steps as you think about what goes into building a practice of forgiveness in your marriage. Think about those three essential materials used to construct the archaic steps that have stood the test of time.

Let's say the stones represent justice. You both have an innate sense of what is morally right and wrong. True forgiveness doesn't throw away your sense of justice. You don't just ignore the emotions from injustice—your feelings of anger, betrayal, and sorrow that rise up when you've been wronged. If you've been wronged, the real story and its moral import are undeniably vital. It isn't authentic to brush offenses to the side as if they're irrelevant facts or to make excuses or to dismiss the reality of your hurt. It's fitting for justice to be represented by stone in these steps because you intuitively know the stones are essential.

What does the mortar represent? Let's say the mortar is mercy. In other words, unearned or unmerited favor. You won't be able to request and wholeheartedly grant forgiveness without a compassionate, undeservedly favorable perspective toward your spouse's weaknesses and errors, and frankly your own too.

To build your forgiveness steps, the third ingredient you need is water. Without water, the mortar isn't pliable or useful for the purpose. No stones are cemented together without it. A posture of humility is the water that makes an ongoing practice of forgiveness possible. It is humility that says, "I'm not better than my spouse. I might not have the same shortcomings, but my shortcomings are not better or worse. There are beautiful *and* unsightly things inside both of us. My mistakes and my weaknesses are hurtful to my spouse, just as my spouse's are hurtful to me." With a spirit of humility, we can recognize and appreciate our common human condition and see each other with compassion.

Justice, mercy, and humility. With these three essential ingredients, you can build practices of forgiveness that will take you to monumental places and create a union so strong that it will endure for years to come.

As I said earlier, forgiveness is not a once-and-done deal. You won't reach your potential together without exercising forgiveness time and time again. Moving forward in your struggling marriage requires both building the steps of forgiveness—building a practice of forgiveness between you—and *using* those steps. Walking them. Over and over and over.

To lead us into a fuller understanding of what true forgiveness is made of, let's look more closely at each of the three essential building materials.

THE STONES OF JUSTICE

Our inclination to care about right versus wrong is innate; we can't ignore justice. However, if caring about justice leads us to set ourselves up as the judge who has the final say, our marriages suffer in a serious way.

In a chapter on forgiveness, why am I starting with justice? Because when there's a wrong committed between two people, let's say a moral injustice, there's a threat that the relationship may break down. Anger is a natural emotional response when someone does something that damages a relationship. Maybe the wrong committed against you was an innocent mistake, but you feel angry anyway. Maybe your spouse's words or behavior triggered something in you because of your past; the words or actions didn't seem offensive to your spouse, but you perceived them as a threat. Perhaps your perception and heightened emotions are the result of a wrong done by someone else, long before this relationship. But you still feel that anger toward the spouse standing before you now—though the true source comes from somewhere else entirely. My point is that anger, resentment, and contempt between married people are complicated, and these emotions can come from various root causes and may be challenging to untangle. The problem arises when you've set yourself up to be the judge of what is morally right and what is morally wrong between you and your spouse—because your judgments will be clouded by your emotions.

I've been there. Here's another way I could have started this conversation about the stones of injustice: Hi, my name is Toni, and I'm an addict. A grievance addict, that is. I overfocus on my own sense of justice. I'm at risk of focusing on what I believe is right and wrong and allowing my judgment between the two to rule my emotions. But here's the problem with that: I tend to view justice through an overly narrow lens. My narrow view of justice puts me at risk of judging my spouse and remaining blind to my own moral faults and weaknesses.

Take this example. Years ago, after we recognized our marriage was in trouble, Carey and I reached out to a pastor who also provided marriage counseling. As we sat in his office, emotions mounted as we both tried to convey our own versions of how we'd been hurt by the other.

After listening to us for a while, our counselor turned to Carey and asked, "You're feeling alone in your marriage, aren't you?" Carey was suddenly so overcome with sorrow, his body collapsed into a fetal position on the floor. And me? I saw it all unfold, but as if I were disconnected and watching from a distance. My heart wasn't moved with compassion. Over Carey's sobs, my inner voice pushed back at the counselor, *Yeah, but if only you saw how he treats me. If he would just stop doing what he does and stop saying what he says, then he wouldn't feel alone.*

Fast-forward several years to when we were holding a dinner party at our home with two couples who were close friends of ours. They knew all about the struggles we were having. Though Carey wasn't sure he was up to entertaining that evening, I felt I needed our friends' company and insisted on hosting anyway. As the evening went on, we hadn't even finished the main course when Carey rose from the table. Without a word he left our guests, went to our bedroom, and shut the door. Instead of my heart being moved with compassion, I felt annoyed at how he'd suddenly bailed on dinner. I still felt as though I was the one who was on the morally right side of the justice scale. If there was just cause for Carey's emotional suffering, and the cause didn't emanate from me, then it must be on him.

One of the guys went to check on him before I did. When I finally went in, the look from his swollen eyes said it all—*You don't even care, do you?*

At that moment, as he searched my eyes for some compassion, I was transported back to the counselor's office and remembered the coldness of my heart. It struck me that years later, my heart had moved so little. It was stone cold, and it was painful for me to see.

These two scenarios, bound together by the depth of Carey's sorrow about our relationship, threw into sharp relief the futility of my stubborn but misguided belief that Carey's suffering was his own fault. I started to see that my attitude was wrong. My belief that I was the victim of injustice at his hands was distorted, and my mindset was hurting us. After all, who set me up to be the judge?

This posture was opposed to the faith I ascribed to. In that moment, I saw how much my overblown judgments and unforgiveness had left me cold and hardened. Maybe some of Carey's behavior that I was labeling as aggressive and "not right" came from a place deep inside him that was desperate, and maybe he had good reason to be desperate. He longed for me to be present with him and not withdrawn. Could what I judged as undue aggression have been Carey's passionate pursuit to have a real connection? To soften my hard heart? As long as I believed that I held the moral upper hand, we would not be able to heal and grow closer.

What about you? Will you search your heart to see whether

you've developed a mindset that always has justice slanting in your favor? Is there a part of you that wants to be the judge? Have you constructed an imbalance of justice that your spouse will never be able to correct? Because if you, like me, see yourself perpetually as a victim of injustice and also as the judge, your heart will grow colder, and the two of you may not be able to overcome this barrier. Your spouse can't decide to shift your perspective and move your stone heart for you. That's something only you can do.

To be clear, paying attention to right and wrong is critically important. When I threw my coffee at Carey, regardless of the content of our argument, I had wronged him, and it was on me to own up to my offense and apologize. Not only that, but I also needed to make it right by cleaning his jacket and the car. If you and your spouse make an agreement on your budget and you blow it with a single purchase, your spouse may rightly look to you to make restitution. Your spouse will look for you to show remorse. If one of you turns outside your marriage for sexual comfort when you've promised fidelity to each other, the other will feel morally outraged for good reason.

Clients whose marriages had broken down after being cheated on would meet with me, still reeling after the sting of betrayal. Meeting after meeting, they would try to redirect my focus to the photos, texts, credit card statements, and everything else they'd collected to prove their spouses were cheating. Although I made it clear they didn't need to prove the affair to me, they seemed driven to prove that they had been wronged—and, for many, driven to see that their spouses should pay. Given the no-fault divorce system we have in Canada, it was my job to sit with my distraught clients and their emotions and gently break to them the reality of the legal limitations. Our system would not exact their version of justice. The legal proceedings wouldn't be capable of, morally speaking, righting the wrongs.

I think it helps to recognize the different approaches to serving justice. One approach says the offender must pay—"an eye for an eye." We expect a judge and perhaps a jury to condemn the wrong that was done and mete out a penalty the offender must pay. This is retributive justice.

But there's another view of justice—a restorative one. The goal of the restorative approach isn't to mete out punishment but rather to recognize the harm of the offense and involve the victim in the problem-solving, including the decision about what would make restitution for the harm done. This approach focuses on real healing, reconciling relationships, and repairing the fabric of the relationships involved.[1]

Do you believe you've been wronged in your marriage? Maybe you actually have been. Maybe, as is true for many couples, the offenses have been mutual. Is there any part of you that looks for your spouse to pay you back for the wrongs you believe he or she has committed against you? Is it possible that you may be judging your spouse, as I did mine, with a distorted view of justice? Underneath your spouse's behavior, could there be a soul longing to be seen and a heart longing for real love? Would a restorative approach to justice serve both of you better?

If you hold on to unforgiveness because deep down you still believe justice demands it, because your spouse does not seem sorry for the wrong committed, you may very well end up going your separate ways. I saw many couples who split because each spouse was convinced he or she had been morally wronged by the other, and each spouse held a view of justice that was immovable.

Just as real as the stones in a staircase are the facts that make up the rights and wrongs between you. The wrongs give rise to real emotions as well. In the spirit of peacemaking, you may choose to overlook the inconsequential injustices. But if what you *really* want is a stronger bond, you both need to acknowledge the noticeable offenses. If you've offended your partner, your first step is to pick up the stone, be real about it, and own it instead of turning a blind eye or wishing it wasn't there.

THE MORTAR OF MERCY

The second essential ingredient of forgiveness is mercy.

Riley and Erika had a profound struggle on their hands when it came to mercy.

"My kids are really angry at me," Riley told me. "Rachel won't see me because she thinks I'm the 'bad guy' who broke up the family. I know Erika tells the kids everything."

Riley and Erika had been married fourteen years. For the first few years, things were good and they had a solid marriage. When their children, Rachel and Joey, were born, Erika decided to stay home to raise them. This arrangement worked while the kids were younger, but once they were in school full-time, Riley wanted Erika to find a job to help with the family's expenses. As a manager at a local bank, Riley was committed to his role as the breadwinner, but trying to make ends meet with his salary alone was challenging. Erika, wanting to be home to be there for the kids before and after school, dismissed the idea of returning to the workplace. But she also wasn't interested in budgeting and tended to lose track of her spending, which only caused more financial stress.

When the children were preschoolers, Erika had started to struggle with anxiety and mild depression and began drinking the occasional glass of wine. But the occasional glass increased to two or three, and sometimes more. Riley dropped hints about her cutting back or, better yet, going sober. But Erika's wine habit became a touchy subject. Her drinking made her irritable and more susceptible to angry outbursts. Sometimes she struggled to get out of bed in the morning to get the kids ready for school. By the time Riley returned home from work, Erika was too numb and distant to have a real conversation with him. As the years passed, they drifted apart, their physical intimacy ended, and the fun times disappeared. Riley spent most of his time around Erika feeling as if he was walking on eggshells.

Riley tried to get the two of them to marriage counseling, but Erika went to one session and left in a rage when the conversation turned to her drinking habit. She said the dynamic was two against one and she wasn't going back.

One thing led to another. Riley's college friend Sophie reached out to him on Facebook. She lived just forty-five minutes from him. After messaging back and forth, they met in a local coffee shop for old times' sake and a chance to catch up on what their other college friends had been up to.

To Riley, the contrast between the dark cloud of his marriage and his lighthearted conversation with Sophie was striking. Emotions that hadn't been stirred in him for a while were sparked again. And there it started. Riley found himself involved with Sophie, in an affair he hadn't been looking for, living the double life of secrecy that left him both exhilarated and desperately anxious. For months, he couldn't help feeling that disaster was just one slip away.

One of Erika's friends, who was also a friend of Sophie's, gave Erika the tip-off. That day, Erika's drinking started early in the afternoon. Riley knew something was wrong when he saw his belongings strewn across the front lawn. In her distraught state, Erika had already blurted out what she'd heard to the kids, now twelve and nine years old, when they arrived home and questioned the mess.

Their daughter, Rachel, confronted Riley as soon as he walked in the door. "What are you going to do now? Walk out on all of us? You wrecked our family! You betrayed us!"

Joey, their son, was also upset. He was curled up on the couch, silently watching. He didn't spew anger, just tears.

Erika insisted that Riley leave immediately and find somewhere else to stay. Riley was stunned, grasping for a word to speak through the fog of fear and dread. He sputtered out, "I'm sorry. Let's not do anything drastic. Let me stay. I don't have anywhere else to go . . . We'll talk . . ."

Joey ran up to his dad and wrapped his skinny arms around Riley's legs to stop him from walking out. "No, Daddy, I don't want you to leave!"

Erika refused Riley's pleas, peeled Joey away, and pushed Riley, shouting, "Get out!" She grabbed her phone and threatened to call the police if he didn't voluntarily leave. Not wanting his children to see more of a scene, Riley kissed Joey, who was sobbing, and walked out.

How could Riley and Erika even *approach* mercy when the pain was overwhelming and the emotions raw? Is there a tougher job for the mortar of mercy than holding together two shattered hearts?[2] Even if the offenses committed against you have mounted to the point where you doubt your marriage is viable, you are not past the point of needing to pick up the mortar of mercy. I don't say this with a spirit of rebuke or rah-rah victory or legalism or perfectionism, but rather I want you to be able to enter your grief, take the mortar in your hands, and build the steps of forgiveness that lead you toward a glorious unburdening of your soul.

Your burden of hurt may make you wonder, *How is mercy even possible?* First, let's talk about what mercy is. As I mentioned earlier, mercy is unmerited or unearned favor. Mercy is leniency toward a debt, which allows you to say to the person who hurt you, "You don't owe me." Mercy is like the generosity of a soul that says, "You've done nothing to earn my favor—quite the opposite—but I'm extending it to you anyway." Why? For the sake of love. You extend mercy for the sake of loving your spouse while allowing his or her faults to fall to the ground, out of sight. For the sake of recognizing that it may have been your spouse who wronged you this time but it's only a matter of time until you wrong your spouse.

Lewis Smedes, who wrote influentially on the topic of forgiveness, tells a fable about "magic eyes." In his fable, a righteous husband lived with bitter hatred toward his wife, who cheated on him. It was only after "he began to see her as a needy woman who loved him instead of a wicked woman who betrayed him" that his heart became free enough to allow her back in.[3] What if this was how you viewed your spouse?

Mercy helps you see your spouse—even through your hurt—as weak and fallible instead of malicious and condemnable.

As Carey and I sat on those church steps, we came face to face with the truth that seeing ourselves and each other through the eyes of mercy would be our only way forward.

Just as it takes time and effort to build steps of forgiveness, it takes time and effort to acquire a fresh vision of your partner. The innate feeling that you are owed something for the unspeakable hurt your spouse caused does not just vanish overnight. What I've said before bears repeating: slow is your friend. It takes time to let go of your instinct to take "an eye for an eye." You need to grieve your hurts and losses. You'll need to be gentle and honest with your spouse and yourself. Rebuilding broken trust will take plenty of time and will require a new track record of loyalty and honesty. Just as stones and water alone won't result in a staircase that lasts for centuries, the practice of forgiveness you build, should you decide to make for higher ground together, won't have the strength required without mutual compassion and mercy.

THE WATER OF HUMILITY

When we've been grievously wronged, the concept of extending forgiveness initially seems like an affront. Without undeserved favor or unmerited compassion—the mortar of mercy—any close relationship draws apart. For mercy to fully do its work, like mortar, it must also be mixed with the water of humility. But Erika, and someone in a similar situation, may not be able to deal with mercy and humility right away. While she's still feeling the intense sting of betrayal, asking her to pick up the mortar of mercy may be inviting her to throw it away. Her husband hurt her, and her reflex is to hurt back. I've seen this striving for justice at work between many separating couples. But given the dignity of time and appropriate attention to the facts as well as to emotions, the essential ingredient of humility changes everything. You see, mercy requires Erika to change the way she looks at what Riley did and who he is; humility requires Erika to change the way she looks at what she did and who she is.

Let's consider what happens when a husband or wife opts to extend mercy without having humility. For example, let's say Riley and Erika went to marriage counseling and eventually decided to give their marriage another try. Riley sincerely apologized and agreed to allow Erika access to his cell phone and computer whenever she asked. Erika said the hard words, "I forgive you." And when she said the words, she thought she meant them.

A little time elapsed, and Erika continued to make random excessive purchases and expected Riley to somehow absorb the impact. She wasn't oblivious to the financial strain she was causing, but rather, underneath her indiscretion was the implicit assumption *You owe me.* Or perhaps, after saying "I forgive you," Erika did nothing to address her drinking habit, and the temperature in the room continued to rise drastically if Riley spoke about it. The implication behind her behavior was that she was entitled to indulge her habits because she held the trump card and he was in her debt.

If this is the case, how will Riley and Erika effectively draw closer to each other while Erika mouths the words of forgiveness but resists the heart posture of humility to own her share of their relational breakdown? You may say that Erika mouthing the words but holding Riley to account in her heart is a failure to extend mercy, and it is; but she's also lacking humility to own her actions that had hurt Riley.

For Riley and Erika to fully restore the closeness between them, Erika needs humility to see how her behavior contributed to the disconnection between them and address it. No doubt, handling mercy in the face of a grievous wrong is hard. For Erika, who's been so hurt, grasping the humility that allows her to see her own part in what led to Riley's affair may be like trying to hold water in her hand. The water of humility may seem to slip through her fingers. But without seeing her own shortcomings, the steps toward real forgiveness cannot be built. At least, not in any lasting way.

Thinking of mercy combined with humility is more apt and more useful when we're talking about building a practice of forgiveness. And mortar mixed with water, ready to use, is a fitting visual picture *because* it's messy. Once you start working with mercy and humility, it's best to do something constructive with it. If you decide to try out the process that may lead you to build the steps to forgive each other and heal, then go as far as you're able. Do your best to build the steps and walk over them.

Consider, is it possible for you to see not only the wrongs done against you but also the wrongs that you have done?

Dr. Martin Luther King Jr. said,

How do we love our enemies? . . . We must recognize that the evil deed of the enemy-neighbor, the thing that hurts, never quite expresses all that he is. An element of goodness may be found in our worst enemy. Each of us is something of a schizophrenic personality, tragically divided against ourselves. A persistent civil war rages within all of our lives. Something within us causes us to lament with Ovid, the Latin poet, "I see and approve the better things, but follow worse," or to agree with Plato that human personality is like a charioteer having two headstrong horses, each wanting to go in a different direction, or to repeat with the Apostle Paul, "The good that I would I do not; but the evil which I would not, that I do."[4]

To forgive, you need to see your spouse through the lens of mercy and see yourself through the lens of humility. I don't think Carey and I would have ever called ourselves enemies, but we sometimes fought as if we were. I had to admit that I didn't come to our marriage whole and pristine—I had to admit that I'm as much a mixture of virtue and brokenness as Carey is. The waters of humility slipped easily through my fingers, too, until I worked harder to hold them in my hand.

building and walking your steps

When you both feel you've been wronged by the other, how do you deal with the tension between acknowledging justice and mixing mercy with humility so you can repair and move on—even if you don't think restoration is possible? How do you build steps of forgiveness out of justice, mercy, and humility? What would that even look like?

Extending mercy must involve acknowledging the offense and engaging your heart in the process. You need to experience, not stuff or deny, your emotions attached to the wrongs. Maybe you need to write down your grievances. Desmond Tutu recommended a ritual of writing the good qualities of the person you're trying to forgive on a stone and then writing the offenses you want to forgive on sand. The offenses will be washed away by the rain, but the truths of the strengths of that person will endure on the rock.[5] This type of ritual is helpful because you'll be able to visualize your act of forgiving. You could also mark your release of each grievance by throwing a stone or shell into an expanse, such as an ocean or lake, or off a cliff, and watch it disappear.[6] Then whenever one of those offenses crosses your mind, you'll be able to picture your prior act of releasing it. It's a way of guarding your heart and your relationship from burdens you already let go of. Once you remove yourself as the judge and relieve yourself of the need to impose the penalty, you may experience an unburdening and a surprising freedom to love.

Maybe you don't want to build the steps to a stronger marriage and you want to split and get a new start, but have you considered what withholding forgiveness will mean for you? Janis Spring, a clinical psychologist and acclaimed expert in the area of intimacy and forgiveness, wrote about the plan to find a "better deal":

> When people get divorced and remarried, they expect to be happier, but the statistics tell a different story. According to leading marital researcher John Gottman, second marriages fail at an even higher rate than first marriages: 50 percent of first marriages and 60 percent of second marriages end in divorce. Add stepchildren, and the number of second marriages that fail jumps to 70 percent. It helps to keep in mind that the happiest couples in America don't resolve some 69 percent of their problems.
>
> When you're deciding whether to leave or to stay and rebuild trust, I encourage you to look beyond the moment and try to see your partner more objectively. For those of you who are swept up by high chemistry, this means seeing past the blind spots of romantic love and opening yourself up to the possibility of a less fiery, but warmer, more lasting love with your partner. . . .
>
> Don't give up on your partner too easily. Ask yourself: "Does the problem lie within our relationship or within me? Have I fallen out of love because my partner can never give me what I need, or because I'm suffering temporarily from the loss of the *illusion* of love: the illusion that seduced

me into believing that love is constant, that I would always feel positively about my partner; that I would never have to struggle with conflicts that made me question our basic compatibility as a couple.[7]

Looking back at that awful "date" night, I realize it could have transpired differently. What if Carey and I had taken time to reflect, done a short workout, listened to music, or done something else to soothe our spirits and lift our moods before we ventured out? What if we'd called it a week and gone to bed early to get some rest? As it was, though, the stark place we ended up showed me my glaring need to start the process of building steps of forgiveness, even if the task would be strenuous and messy. If our marriage was going to make it, I had to get serious about forgiving and asking for forgiveness. It was the only way we would share a satisfying relationship, bonded securely and not weighed down by burdens of resentment.

I needed to forgive Carey for his words and actions that hurt me, and I needed to confess and ask for forgiveness for my own offenses. I had to add humility to my willingness to extend mercy. I needed to listen to his perspectives and own up to the harm that I had caused. I had to discard my misguided concepts of who was right and who was wrong so we could repair and move on. I needed to practice confessing—to be specific about what wrong I was asking Carey to forgive me for.

Many years later, our steps of forgiveness have well-worn tracks. As we've committed to mixing those three ingredients, our hearts are more intertwined. We're closer than we've ever been.

Are you willing to invest time, effort, and sweat to construct steps of forgiveness? Are you willing to use the approaches of prayer, mediation, and self-reflection? Are you willing to build forgiveness with the steps made from justice, mercy, and humility? After you take the building materials and construct the steps, will you make the effort to climb them and not just stare passively at them? I hope that sooner rather than later the forgiveness steps you build will take you somewhere awe-inspiring together and receive their due glory.[8]

FIND WHAT YOU *REALLY* WANT

1. Would you say the model of justice you grew up with was more restorative or more retributive? What factors did you consider in your answer?
2. When you make an apology to your spouse, what helps convince him or her that you're sincere?
3. Has there ever been a time when you've struggled to forgive someone? Describe how justice, mercy, and humility have shown up in the process, even if your steps of forgiveness aren't fully finished yet.

PART 3

toward your way better future

CHAPTER 9

don't play it safe

I instinctively wrapped my arms around my son Jordan's soaked body and drew his head toward my chest to comfort him and quiet his frightened cries. The blackness blanketed us both. I lifted him out of the bath with one arm while groping for a towel with the other. Not even a sliver of light made its way through the cracks around the bathroom door. The force of the summer storm pummeled the walls and windows, causing our house to lose power. I'd heard the wind hiss around aging window frames with muffled thunder in the background, but losing power hadn't really crossed my mind. For my toddler-aged son, this thick darkness set to the soundtrack of the raging storm turned his splashing fun into something horrific.

After that night, Jordan refused to take a bath. What had been one of his favorite pastimes became a thing of terror. No amount of coaxing, cajoling, demanding, or even bribing would convince our toddler otherwise. For weeks, we had to resort to "baths" in the kitchen sink, plus the occasional swim at the local rec center.

One day it struck me that to get different results would require a different approach. That afternoon I gathered up plastic boats and floaty toys, dumped them in the bathtub, and ran the water. I didn't say a word about having a bath. Jordan stared at me with wide eyes as he peeked around the pedestal sink and watched as I stepped into the bath with all my clothes on. I sat down to play. As I raced the plastic boat from one end to the other, he took a step closer. As I bobbed it up and down, creating waves, he looked on curiously. Then he moved forward and stretched his dimpled arms over the bathtub edge to grab for the boat. Eager for his toys, he climbed over the edge and picked up a ball with one hand and a rubber duck with the other. He plunked himself down with a splash.

"Hey, we're having fun!" I said, hiding a smirk. He barely noticed while I slowly took off his shirt and socks and got the soap out. His terror had vanished.

There are times when words are not enough. Helping Jordan overcome the traumatic bathtub memory with my words didn't work. No matter how insistent or persuasive, whatever I said didn't loosen the grip of fear. Jordan didn't need reassuring, coaxing, or healing words. He needed a leader. He needed to see me go first.

We've discussed a lot of problems that could be at the core of why you feel stuck in your marriage. But there is a barrier that you and your spouse may be facing that runs deeper than strong emotions when it comes to saving a marriage. If you've digested the messages of the earlier chapters and still feel unsure of the way out of unhappiness, the barrier is probably not your lack of information or knowledge. You at least have a clue as to what your marriage problems are. And you're probably able to identify your next step toward progress for at least one of those problems. In fact, you may even have a menu of next steps that your rational brain assents to, and you wouldn't go wrong choosing any one of them. They're all good options for initiating change.

No, if you've been struggling, the barrier that is holding you back is something deeper than strong emotions or a lack of information. The problem at its core is this: you're stuck in your marriage because neither of you trusts the other enough to be the one to take the first step toward real and lasting change—which ulti-

mately requires risk and humility. And with that first step, someone needs to keep moving forward with consistency. You don't
trust your spouse deep down, and that feeling is mutual. Something in you doesn't want to be the first to put yourself out there.
The initial few moments and days and weeks of change are messy,
confusing, and hard to handle. To take the first step, you first have
to contend with your own internal battle. You don't know whether
your spouse will reciprocate. Maybe you feel as if you're handing
over a little more power than you wish to part with. Having said
that, there's something in you that wants your marriage to succeed. So are you willing to take the first step anyway? Because
here's a secret: you won't save your marriage by playing it safe.

will you take the lead?

We humans are fascinated with hero stories. Take this scene from
Wonder Woman:[1]

When the enemy forces are poised to release deadly mustard
gas on the unsuspecting residents of Veld, Diana Prince—Wonder
Woman—surveys the small band of would-be rescuers who traveled to the enemy front with her. Who dares venture into No
Man's Land? The marksman? The spy? Whoever steps out in front
to get the base will take the enemy fire. As she evaluates the group
surrounding her, one by one they shrink back. And just in time,
that moment arrives when she has clarity. She sees her calling and
seizes it. With her bracelets around her forearms, she dons her tiara
and finds the courage to step out and risk taking the hits. Her decision is vital to the advance. Only after she moves forward do the
allied forces rise up behind her. A trained warrior herself, Diana
knows that without a leader, there is no chance of victory.

You may feel you aren't a natural-born leader. Most of us won't
be at the front lines of a military battle. You may never have led an
organization, a nonprofit, or a team. Or maybe you have, but

whatever leadership role you played felt well supported and didn't demand a lot of courage. In those circumstances, leading doesn't feel like much of a risk. But even if you find Wonder Woman's willingness to step out into danger somewhat surreal, I urge you to focus on one discreet part of her narrative: that is, Diana Prince's steadfast commitment to the end goal that gives rise to her decision to override her doubts and fears with action. She realizes that to make change, save lives, and advance the cause, someone must go first. In that moment, she influences the people around her by taking one step. You may be skeptical about everything hinging on a momentary decision, but sometimes it does. In your community, your family, and your marriage, you are an influencer. Exerting influence by taking a step, saying the difficult words, or responding to circumstances that need adjusting is a form of leadership—a type of leadership that isn't restricted to those with a natural gifting but is open to us all.[2]

You may object to being called on to take a first step toward healing your marriage because you feel you've already done it and so far it hasn't worked. You may think, *I've been taking the lead to get our budget under control for years.* Or, *I'm already taking more of the lead in our marriage by assuming the responsibilities of managing our family and all the kids' needs, but my leading hasn't made us happier.* That's not the kind of leading I'm talking about. I'm not referring to leading in the management of your home or your family. And I'm not referring to the type of leading that is "bossing around"—threatening, cajoling, or withholding.

I'm not using the term *leader* in the sense of "ruler" or "autocrat" or "benevolent dictator." I'm using it to mean a person who is willing to serve others with the gifts and influence they have. Back to Wonder Woman: She wore the Bracelets of Submission, which symbolized strength balanced by love. She explained that a leader who is strong will abuse her power unless she's bound by love. A leader bound by love is one committed to using the power she has to empower someone else, to serve someone else. What role might that type of leadership play in transforming your marriage?

In these next few pages, consider these traits that give leaders influence so you have the opportunity to see some of them in yourself. Your decision to lean into even one of them might help you grow personally, and in doing so you may positively influence your relationship with your spouse. The truth is that you have more capacity for growth than you might have thought possible. But you can also ignore the influence you have and sabotage your opportunity to grow into a more loving version of yourself. Whether or not you do is entirely up to you.

We humans get ourselves into all kinds of situations that require real courage to take the first step. Taking that step into the potential line of fire is scary—especially when the two of you are already struggling. You might be tempted not to take any risks because you think, *I don't want any part of a sham of a marriage, and that's exactly what my marriage feels like. Wouldn't I be a fool to expect anything different for the future?* Or you may think, *What if I admit I was wrong and I get shut down, embarrassed, or rejected?* Or you may wonder just how many seeds of kindness you have to sow while your spouse doesn't return the favor. You might be wondering if you have it in you to be persistent and patient.

Let's set aside these questions and try to keep an open mind. Why don't we examine a few leadership traits? Adopting even one may help you through the No Man's Land of your marriage.

trait #1: leaders take risks

A key quality of a leader is that he or she is willing to make a decision and be the first to step out, for better or for worse. Even when the move seems wise and has been thought out, a leader understands there is the chance of success and the risk of failure. To apply this to marriage, the spouse who's willing to take the first step must also be willing to serve the other in love, and so I'll call the spouse who takes initiative the "servant leader."

In this way, the servant leader husband or wife is the one willing to risk being emotionally open and vulnerable when the response from the other side may very well be hostile. A servant leader husband or wife is

- the one willing to humbly make the apology first,

- the one who makes the choice to do the loving thing while his or her emotions are pulling in the opposite direction, and

- the one who recognizes the subtle insult and doesn't respond in retaliation.

Carey and I have very different love languages. In case you haven't heard about love languages, your love language is the primary way that love is communicated to or received by you as an individual. Dr. Gary Chapman has identified five of them: acts of service, words of affirmation, physical touch, gifts, and quality time.[3] Chances are, your love language and your spouse's are not the same. Quality time is what speaks to me, while Carey's primary love language is acts of service. While I value all kinds of labor, that doesn't mean I like doing it—housework is an example of that. Yet cleaning our house, keeping the closets in order, and washing the cars are ways for me to communicate love to Carey in a way he naturally receives it.

What do love languages have to do with taking risks? The risk shows up in how I spend my time. I see my time as precious, and I bet you see yours that way too. I typically don't want to spend more time than necessary cleaning the house—I see it as simply a means to an end. So going the extra mile to organize the toolbox or clean off the shelves in the garage is something I would avoid, *except* for the sake of love. When I do those types of things, I'm giving away my time. When my relationship is struggling and I'm not sure how my spouse will respond to my act of service, I'm taking a risk with it. But if I choose not to take that risk, I'm missing an opportunity to show love.

When I first chose to spend time on acts of service that I knew Carey would appreciate, I needed to dismiss the thought that I was wasting my time doing more chores than necessary. Rather, I did it for the sake of rebuilding our connection.

What about risks beyond lost time? If you are the one who leads in turning around your marriage, you may face other types of loss. Maybe you'll lose the opportunity to do other activities or pursue other friendships, even temporarily. You might risk loss of relationships (with people who aren't supportive), financial loss (considering the expense of professional services, for example), or personal loss (if the time you invest in solving your marriage problems comes at the expense of something else, such as time at the gym). Just as Wonder Woman chanced the stray bullet as she stepped out, you chance some emotional hits when you take a risky step toward resolving the problems between you and your spouse. The hits I'm referring to could involve temporarily intensifying the emotional pain you may already be familiar with. To be clear, I'm not referring to physical pain or emotional abuse. I'm referring to the pain of sacrificing your desire or swallowing your pride or holding your tongue. This setting-aside-your-ego pain is the price of progress.

What scary step could turn the trajectory of your relationship? Out of the countless options, here are a few examples. Let's say you've been the driving force behind some altercations between the two of you, but you've never been able to bring yourself to say, "I hurt you when I did this thing, and I was wrong. Will you please forgive me?" Admitting you were wrong is difficult because it might feel like opening the floodgates. Dread holds you back. Maybe you feel admitting *this* wrong means admitting you have something fundamentally wrong with you at your core. It can feel true even when it isn't. Maybe you've been withholding a secret you've never disclosed and the pressure you feel inside keeps mounting. It's making you resent your spouse. He or she doesn't even get the chance to respond with compassion because you've already written off your spouse as untrustworthy. Or maybe you recognize the financial pressure you're both facing, but taking that first step toward the workplace seems too daunting. Can you accept working in a position that seems to underrepresent your skill set and still preserve your dignity? What would your friends think?

Maybe in each of these scenarios, viewing yourself as a *servant* leader would help you take the risk. To help you with the first step, ask yourself, *By taking this risk to serve my spouse, is it possible that my spouse will respond with love? Will my spouse eventually come around and serve me too?*

It may be less intuitive to view marriage as a relationship where the goal is to serve each other's needs and desires instead of a relationship where each spouse sets the bar at a certain height and expects the other to clear it. The former is a recipe for love and peace; the latter is a formula for relational injury. If both people in a marriage throw themselves into the risk of becoming a servant leader to the other, stand back and watch what happens. The shaky relationship of two individuals each fighting for his or her own self-interest morphs into a relationship with solid footing. Words and actions of service communicate more caring. More caring leads to more relational satisfaction. More satisfaction leads to more playfulness and fun. What started with serving ends up producing more passionate love. And when two people carry out the commitment to serve each other in love over time, eventually the marriage becomes a wonder to behold.

How about being the first to take the risk in your marriage? You don't need to have a cooperative partner, and you don't even need to feel like doing it. You can take a lot of first steps on your own, starting with your decision to take a risk to turn your marriage around.

trait #2: leaders are biased toward action

Henry Ford once said, "Most people think that faith means *believing* something; oftener it means *trying* something, giving it a chance to prove itself."[4]

Chances are, you have friends or acquaintances who are all talk and no action. At first, their ideas seemed credible. Maybe the new businesses or the ventures they were talking about sounded intriguing. But as talk continued over time with no action, your view of your friends and their plans became clouded with cynicism. For good reason—because eventually you could see clearly that your friends weren't making any progress, and all the plans they'd talked about amounted to nothing. They were confusing intention with action.

When it comes to saving a marriage, it's overly easy to get stuck in all talk and no action. We're all naturally self-protective. Sometimes we fail to take steps toward progress because we listen too intently to the voices of pride and fear.

Pride says, "My way is better." It motivates you to refuse to stand in the shoes of your spouse and attempt to see the world through his or her eyes. It falsely believes that there's something deviant or deficient about your spouse's different perspective. Or pride resists seeing your spouse's viewpoint because doing so would mean you might support a view you've previously fought against. Pride hates to be humble and admit that it was wrong.

Fear says things like "I'm afraid of being taken advantage of" or "I don't want to become a doormat" or "I'll give things up and get nothing in return" or "If I don't protect myself, no one will."

When you and your spouse are struggling, you may not even be aware of how you're protecting your pride or responding to your fears and anxieties—while their internal messages may be altogether false with no grounding in reality.

When you're in favor of saving your marriage but you're not

actually *trying out* something new or extending yourself somehow, then you might be stuck in inaction. You may have good intentions and your interactions with your spouse are decent or civil, but if you aren't taking concrete steps that will move you closer together, do you think it might be time to make a move?

For Carey and me, one factor that kept us stuck for so long may have been my own failure to move to deal with my anxiety and depression. The emotional clues weren't invisible to me; I recognized my struggle, but fear paralyzed me from picking up the phone or doing anything that would lead me into unfamiliar territory. For years, dark moods and deep sadness washed over me in waves and would lift just enough so I could say I was okay. If only I had taken these signs seriously and consulted with a professional earlier and more consistently, I—and our whole family—would have been better off. Once I took the step of talking to my physician about how I was really feeling and then started treatment and counseling, I was able to make real progress. How I was showing up in our marriage improved dramatically. I believe that if I'd had made an attempt sooner to take action to solve my mood problems, Carey and I may have been spared some of our grief.

If you see in you any part of my natural tendency to be too accepting of the status quo or to confuse thinking about doing something with actually doing it, what would it take to develop more of a bias toward action? What is it you need to do that you haven't done yet? Make that apology? Get out the vacuum and clean up the dog hair? Suggest a date over breakfast? Drive to the store and buy some truffles? Overhaul the budget? Sign you both up for the gym (with the consent of your spouse, of course)? You have no idea what hangs in the balance when you decide to act.

Put your plan for your next step into motion. Your path to your better relationship goes nowhere unless you decide to move.

trait #3: leaders are tenacious

In the movie *Christopher Robin,*[5] Winnie the Pooh enters the tree house of his former forest home, alive with the memories of the long-ago adventures he'd had with his friends Tigger, Eeyore, Piglet, and, of course, Christopher Robin. To Pooh's amazement, the tree house becomes a passageway to the garden beside Christopher Robin's house. He is saddened to find his friend, now an adult with his own family, burdened by his obsession with work. Christopher Robin is unable to focus on the family who loves him. Pooh then has a mission—find the childhood version of Christopher Robin he knew and loved. To do so, Pooh faces many obstacles:

- Christopher Robin has grown cold and distant; he seems to have forgotten their affectionate friendship.

- Pooh is alone in the forest; he doesn't know where his friends have gone.

- The condition of the forest has deteriorated and is scary.

- Pooh has no idea how to accomplish his mission.

Winnie the Pooh must keep his eyes focused on his mission and not allow himself to be defeated by these barriers or his disappointment, his fear, his sadness, or anything else. In other words, he has to have tenacity, which Merriam-Webster's dictionary defines as "the mental or moral strength to resist opposition, danger, and hardship."[6]

You already know that leading any kind of change is challenging, and chances are, you've already had to garner up some tenacity when it comes to your marriage. However, maybe you're like me. Maybe you go through days or seasons where you'd welcome more mental or moral strength—a little more of that superpower that would enable you to push through opposition and hardship for a worthy cause.

If that's true, I encourage you to look at tenacity a different way. See it not as a superpower you lack but as a source of strength you already have access to that helps keep your eyes focused on the bigger picture. A great analogy for tenacity, related to planting and harvesting, comes from ancient wisdom: "Those who go out weeping, carrying seed to sow, will return with songs of joy, carrying sheaves with them."[7] This refers to restoring good fortune, not now but in the future. It isn't clear what type of crop is being sown, where, or by whom. But one thing we do know: where there's weeping, there's sorrow. I imagine the author saw the breadth of human misery and took at least half a lifetime to observe what happened to those who planted seeds during their grief. Despite their sorrows, the people carry the seeds into the fields and plant them. To plant seeds despite hardship, which could be famine or loneliness or illness or oppression, requires these people to take action *while* they're suffering, with no promise of any immediate benefit. There is no instant reward to lessen the grief. The people must wait and—in the waiting—not give up hope.

Why plant the seeds when there are tears and sorrow and hardship? Because there's the *promise* of a harvest, and not only that but there's the promise of abundance, symbolized by the sheaves. And the promise is not only for the rich reward of the harvest but also for the songs of joy. This ancient wisdom invites you to fix your eyes on the abundant future rewards of the harvest and joy that will result from your seed planting. Taking steps while you're suffering requires a mental fortitude, for sure, but that fortitude is not exclusive or a superpower you don't have access to. You can do this too.

Tenacity and the principles of the harvest have something to say about taking the lead to help save your marriage. The principles of the harvest say that you reap *what* you sow, you reap *later* than you sow, and you reap *more* than you sow.[8]

YOU REAP *WHAT* YOU SOW

Are you sowing seeds of kindness, patience, and love? Or are you sowing indifference, criticism, or suspicion? What is the quality and nature of your words and actions—the seeds you're sowing—in your relationship? Don't be worried about the size of the seeds. Every little kindness, every little gift, every small apology, and every overlooking of a slight have the potential to create results that vastly outgrow what you planted. Remember that a tiny mustard seed can give birth to a splendidly spacious tree.

YOU REAP *LATER* THAN YOU SOW

Don't expect instant results when you start planting the seeds of new life in your marriage. Have willingness to wait. Anyone who's had experience with planting knows it's futile to keep your eyes fixed on the spot where you planted. Don't plant the seeds of generosity and kindness and then watch your spouse to measure the response. You'll only set yourself up for disappointment if you expect your partner to spring into action once you've extended yourself for him or her. Watching doesn't make the seed grow faster. But fastening your hope to the promise of your harvest and your joy in the future will make the waiting easier.

YOU REAP *MORE* THAN YOU SOW

Your grace-filled attitude toward your spouse and your new, loving habits will have a cumulative impact over time. People and marriages may sometimes appear static, but they really aren't. A marriage is either building and growing or deteriorating and declining. Habits of love consistently practiced between two people over time will build into a deeper and more abundant relationship. You have the potential to build a richly satisfying future marriage by sowing the seeds of love now—even if you have to sow the seeds into hard ground. Bitterness and indifference accumulate over time too, and they do so in such a way that sucks the life and joy out of those involved. Carried on over time, these destroy both self and others.

Even if your partner doesn't reciprocate while you've been planting seeds, *you will reap a harvest* when you authentically sow seeds of love and keep on sowing. The harvest may not appear where you intended, but the promise stands, and you will experience a reward that is worth the wait.

The harvest I'm referring to here is the richness of your relationships, and for our purposes, hopefully that's with your spouse. But it could equally be deeper and livelier relationships you experience with your children, your friends, and your other family members when you focus on growing in your capacity to love people. If you and your spouse end up splitting after you've put yourself out there and invested your time, effort, and resources, you may think that you will have lost your chance of future reward, but that's simply not true. You stand to only gain, not lose, by becoming a more loving version of yourself. You'll be prepared for a more joy-filled future. That's how being tenacious becomes a gift to you.

do you have the courage to serve?

Don't fool yourself into thinking that the principle of the harvest is too complicated or that it helps others but won't help you. I remember a time in our marriage when I might have thought that, but our experience proved me wrong.

I remember once when Carey and I were in an argument, I

looked away from him to stare out the living room window. I surveyed the silhouette of our neighbor's barn across the way, black against the ink-blue twilight sky. It was such a familiar sight, having stood unchanged over the eleven years that we had lived in this hamlet of rural Ontario.

I found myself whisper-yelling my retorts to Carey. Angry, but not wanting to rouse our kids with our raised voices, I wrestled my voice down. Then all the competing emotions in me spilled over each other and blended into a bland numbness that had no more words to speak.

Should I ignore what Carey is saying? I wondered. *Should I walk away and focus on something more constructive?* I didn't know how to engage in our differences anymore. I wondered whether I should reach out and let the people close to us know how deeply we were struggling. *Should I get our counselor on the phone and ask for help? Or how about just driving away?* I let the force of my feelings spill over my face as I sat there weeping in a daze.

In the middle of our living room, Carey turned toward me. When I became emotionally overwhelmed and moved into my own little world away from him, he usually tried to push back. What he said next did just that. Of all the seeds we've planted in our marriage since the drought years, this one perhaps carried with it the greatest promise. Carey drew a deep breath, looked into my eyes, and said, "You know what? You deserve better than this. You deserve someone who cherishes you. And cherishing you is what I'm going to focus on from now on."

I was stunned. And the truth was, I didn't really deserve it. I hadn't been very loving, engaged, or available to Carey. I'd had an antagonistic attitude toward him. But Carey stepped away from his dashed expectations and his own hurt, his own disappointment, and his own fear and took a courageous step. He planted the seed through the tears. He chose to set aside his emotions in that moment and decided to serve. He committed to focus on cherishing me.

Since that day, we've lived out the cumulative effects of the moment-by-moment decisions, actions, kindnesses, undeserved acts of forgiveness, and on and on. Tiny seeds have the potential to bear the richest harvest when we keep planting them over time.

You can be the leader your marriage needs. But it takes courage. Don't play it safe. Take a risk. Act. Be tenacious. Plant seeds for a rich marriage harvest, and hold out for joy.

FIND WHAT YOU *REALLY* WANT

1. How has distrust for your partner shown up in your marriage, either now or in the past? If you've made progress in this area, how did you become more trusting?
2. Think of someone you know who, while being sensitive to his or her own needs, serves his or her spouse well. What can you apply from that person's way of leading?
3. What action step has the potential to turn the trajectory of your relationship?

CHAPTER 10

find the fun and intimacy
you've been missing

In the beginning of our marriage, Carey and I laughed and played a lot. We would occasionally go on an adventure for a couple of days, staying at a farm or cottage. We'd spend slow time with friends, practicing artsy photography and exploring the surroundings with no particular goal. We'd go to a comedy show or to hear a local musician. We had spontaneous fun, such as having tickle fights or building a snowman. And I'd sometimes wait around a corner to startle Carey—a fun way to make him laugh. But those lighthearted, playful moments seemed to be overtaken by all the serious things once our family life was in full swing.

When we reached the point where we could hardly stand being in the same room together, having fun didn't seem feasible. It was easier to allow work, kids' activities, homework, church, and family events to fill our calendars and distract us from thoughts about the fun we weren't having. We knew we needed to make *some* effort to stay connected, so we kept our date nights going even when we didn't feel like spending more time together. For a while, they were rough. For the most part, "date night" was "fight night." But we determined to stick with it.

Although our relationship was struggling, we found we were still able to experience fun and laughter together when we had company: going on double dates, watching a comedy with the family, or laughing with a crowd at a party. But the truth is, it took deliberate and persistent baby steps to make it back to having fun times with just the two of us. We learned that sharing a few good moments amid a challenging season could go a long way toward fostering hope for our future.

One of these times for us was a weekend getaway at a picturesque Heritage Inn while our kids were in the care of trusted family members. The first evening, Carey and I remained quiet, but dining by candlelight on a white linen tablecloth set with fine crystal helped us appreciate our time away as a gift. There was something about the serenity, the ambience of the grand restored mansion, and the beautiful nature outside that melted our tension. We left our pressured world and frayed emotions and sank into the haven together. We vowed that we would avoid any hot topics. And during this getaway we found an appetite for fun again. Under the crisp winter sun, we used snowshoes to explore the snowy display of massive pines and granite boulders. And then by the fireside, we delighted in the luxury of lingering over lovemaking. It was an oasis from all our troubles, which helped set our souls' resolve for the work of reconnecting that still lay ahead.

Even if your marriage makes you feel like running away, it's possible to return to fun and intimacy. Making a plan might sound like an unromantic place to start, but hey, what if it works? Though it isn't possible to cover all the ways in one chapter, here are a few strategies that proved helpful for us.

value shared experiences

Sometimes you can get so caught up in your daily routines that you forget how you used to have fun with your spouse. So, what if sharing a new experience could help draw you closer together?

The change you're seeking could start with a conversation about what activities you could do together to try to rebuild your relationship. This isn't about focusing on the work or the *must-do* to fix your marriage; it's about focusing on the fun and *get-to* part of it. We have friends who made up their minds, during a season of deep struggle, to switch their conversation from how to split to how to give their marriage one last try. Their hearts were so disconnected that splitting at that point would have actually felt easier. They mutually decided to watch *one* television show together each week—one they were both interested in. After a while, their television watching led to engaging in another activity together that required more effort and communication. They gradually eased into having a nice dinner out—with the rule that they would avoid contentious topics and keep their conversation focused on the positive. When that proved successful, they started to have more honest and compassionate conversations with each other. Eventually, their safe experiences led to traveling together, sometimes with friends and sometimes just the two of them. That was several years ago. And while they would say they still have their tension points (who doesn't?), they now no longer consider splitting to be an option. They have rebuilt strong bonds, they operate as a team, and they once again enjoy a satisfying relationship. What they're most excited about is that they grew back in love. All because they started with one simple, enjoyable, new experience.

For Carey and me, we agreed to try one thing that the other person found fun. Carey used to not like snowshoeing—something I enjoy—but he agreed to try it with me for the sake of finding something to do together. Now, years later, we both love snowshoeing. And my task was to attempt road cycling with Carey. I had to push past my fear of sharing the road with cars and my aversion to having my shoes clipped into the pedals. The thought of not having my feet free to reach the ground without a thought was daunting. But I agreed to give it a try.

One day we were cycling along a path covered with a fine limestone gravel. While it isn't ideal for the skinny tires of a road bike, the path is a refuge from pickup trucks. When we approached one of our country roads, I slowed to a stop. The problem was that I forgot to swing my heel out to unclip my shoe. As soon as my body leaned to the left, I realized two things: the split second it takes to unclip my shoe was gone, and I was going down. I hit the ground with a thud like a felled tree. Unfortunately, that wasn't the only time that happened—I fell three other times that first season. That part of taking up road cycling obviously wasn't fun, but the pain eventually pushed me through my steep learning curve. My thoughts during my second season of cycling were remarkably consistent: *My feet are clipped, my feet are clipped* . . . Given another chance to do that over, I would have spent more time practicing on grass.

Carey and I now find that cycling together provides fun and beautiful moments to share. We enjoy the exhilaration of zipping down a hill at a speed unmatched by running or kayaking. We love breezing through a grove of lilacs in the spring and through a canopy of trees when trilliums blanket the forest. We may share thoughts or simply take in the natural surroundings in silence.

There was nothing scientific about our agreement to try out each other's idea of fun. But research has shown that if our goal is to establish a more satisfying connection, it helps to pay attention to our emotions around a proposed shared activity. It's worthwhile to distinguish between activities that are "exciting" versus "pleasant." Researchers found that when couples shared an activity they both found "novel or exciting" as opposed to "comfortable or routine" for ninety minutes a week over several consecutive weeks, the excitement or satisfaction they experienced in their relationship measurably increased.[1] Replacing activities that are comfortable with ones that are novel or exciting may build your satisfaction with each other. Carey and I have tried sea kayaking, paddleboarding, and a zip-lining—although exciting doesn't have to mean adrenaline producing. A cooking class is in our near future. How about a clambake or bird-watching? A whole world of experiences is waiting for you.

Now that I've raised fun and intimacy, you might be asking, *What about sex?* This is a difficult subject, especially if you're feeling disconnected or resentful or you're not feeling all that attracted to your spouse. Even when our relationship was a mess, there was never a period of time when Carey and I stopped having sex. But I'll be honest, there were times it was less frequent. We were intentional about our physical intimacy. We didn't want our sexual relationship to become a means to an end, so we both approached our sex life in an aspirational way. We strove to be close and maintain our physical connection as a couple. And even when we were struggling, having sex gave us hope that the other areas of our relationship could become good again. I know from having listened to other people's stories that having sex with each other during challenging times is not a given. I spoke with many clients who hadn't been intimate together in years. Which raises the chicken-and-egg question: Did the relationship break down and *then* they stopped having sex, or did the relationship break down, at least in part, *because* they stopped having sex? Losing your physical connection has the potential to drive you and your spouse further apart.

Prominent psychologists Henry Cloud and John Townsend said this:

> Look up intercourse at www.webster.com, and here is what you find: "(1) connection or dealings between persons or groups, (2) exchange especially of thoughts or feelings, (3) physical sexual contact between individuals that involves the genitalia of at least one person." If couples would just follow the dictionary, things would work out better for them: (1) deal with each other in a way that connects, (2) exchange thoughts and feelings, and (3) go for it![2]

Physical intimacy, honest communication, and your depth of feelings are all connected. There's evidence that oxytocin, the hormone that creates trust and bonding, is released during an orgasm.[3]

So sexual intimacy helps a couple feel closer, form a stronger bond, and feel more satisfied with their partnership. As long as you both agree that sex is something you want, even if you have conflicting emotions, physical intimacy may influence the other efforts you're making to set your marriage on a better path.

If your sex life feels like something less than what you desire, then *please* take steps to figure out why. Are you experiencing problems enjoying your physical intimacy or reaching an orgasm? Are there hurts in your past that are affecting your sexuality? Take courage and reach out to a professional to get the help you need. Talk to your physician if you suspect you or your partner has a physical or emotional condition interfering with your intimacy. If what you *really* want is to stay together, your sexual connection is too important to let it slip away.

focus on your partner's inherent value

Marriage researcher John Gottman stresses that if you want to strengthen your relationship, you should focus on the bond of friendship and the importance of fondness and admiration.[4] I think he's right, but when you've drifted apart or you're feeling disconnected or you have mutual contempt for each other, focusing on the positive may be a proposition you're tempted to shrug off. When the possibility of friendship seems remote and you feel like disengaging, what do you do?

You can start by paying attention to how much positive versus negative communication flows between you. Researcher Dr. Brent J. Atkinson has studied how using positive words can help build a stronger relationship. He highlights the importance of a five-to-one ratio of positivity to negativity in a successful marriage. This means a spouse should express appreciation, affirmation, or another positive emotion, which includes flirting and sharing affection, five times for every one complaint or criticism.[5]

Focusing on the inherent worth in each other was an important part of repairing our emotional intimacy and transforming our marriage, as was our willingness to curb the flow of negative communication and steer more toward the positive.

Maybe the ways you've both responded to your differences have been natural or explainable but have also been counterproductive. You desire a soul mate, but you may seriously doubt your spouse's ability to assist you at all with self-expression or personal growth. Your partner's outlook is just so different from yours.

What if you were able to see the differences between you and your partner as something purposeful and designed rather than as deficiencies?[6] What if your spouse isn't tragically or defectively different from you but wonderfully different? On your journey of moving closer together, what if the next step lies in setting aside your narratives and broken selves and allowing your souls to really see and appreciate the inherent value in each other? This may be a mindset shift that feels impossible. It may take a lot of patience, self-examination, wisdom seeking, counsel, and time to shift your focus from your partner's faults and weaknesses to his or her inherent worthiness. But perhaps your persistence would pay off.

For a recent Christmas, Carey and I decided to travel with our kids to the tropics. Trading parkas and snow clearing for flip-flops and sand seemed like a good idea to everyone. As we strolled through the humid dusk under sheltering palms, what captured my senses was not the inviting temperature (as pleasant as it was) but rather a chirping sound that was lyrical. It had such a striking musical quality to it. If emerald-green-blue Caribbean waters could be transposed into a sound, what we heard might be it. The sound was so magical and perfect, I concluded that the resort had taken notes from Disney and created a soundtrack to enhance the ambience. It was only after a couple of conversations with resort staff that I learned the chirping wasn't fake at all. It wasn't played over hidden speakers. "Might be tree frogs?" guessed a few island dwellers. Sometimes our perceptions of what is true and what is false, what is real and what is fake, can be completely off. We humans tend to jump to our own individual conclusions, but not all of them are accurate. It's so incredibly easy for our perceptions to be skewed. Which leads me to ask: Is it possible that your perceptions of your spouse may not be accurate?

What if your partner's value isn't related to his or her positive attributes and whether they outweigh the negative ones? What if there's no cosmic weigh scale that attempts to measure personal strengths versus weaknesses to equal some unit of worth? What if your perceptions play more of a role than you think? What if your partner's value in your eyes is based on your capacity to perceive value?

Jay Jay is a twelve-year-old miniature poodle. His blue eyes now hold a milky whiteness because he's mostly blind. He moves unusually for a dog as he cranes his neck toward the ceiling to see better. He trips over things and stumbles down steps. He's cantankerous at times. He can't play much anymore, and his woolly coat is seriously sparse on his back. But Jay Jay is also one of the most treasured dogs I know. He is often found cradled in someone's arms like a baby. Jay Jay's value clearly isn't based on any standard of performance—how could it be? His inherent value is displayed by how well and thoroughly he is loved.

If you treat your partner as if he or she has inherent value, would there be more loving feelings between you? I think so. The way you respond to your perception of value speaks volumes in your relationship.

Try working toward being able to say, "[Partner's name] isn't like me but is just as valuable and worthy of love as I am." If you ascribe to a faith, your statement might be "[Partner's name] isn't like me but is made in the image of God. There is something that displays God's glory inside [him or her]." In other words, you recognize that your partner has inherent value, just as you do.

All of us—without exception—have many ways we fall short and mess up. No, your spouse doesn't always get it right. Maybe he keeps avoiding the topic you need to discuss that often ends up in an argument. Maybe she keeps wanting to talk when you feel your own well of words has gone dry. A lot of us have grand-scale personal messes to sort out. But what if you could see the inherent differences between you and your spouse as part of the glory of who you both are designed to be? You have inherent worth, and your spouse does too. Let the love you're seeking be found in the love you offer.[7]

explore how spirituality can help

You may have a faith, or maybe you've had some kind of an experience with faith. It could be that your faith is the foundation for your life. Perhaps you were on a faith journey, but as life became busier, it fell to the side. You may have been disappointed by church people, and as a result you've stayed away from religion, church, and spirituality. It could be that science led you to believe that the answers to the origin of life are found in the natural and not the supernatural. Or you may believe that people of faith portray a God of judgment, which you can't reconcile with a God who is also supposed to be loving. Maybe you already ascribe to a faith but so far it hasn't really helped your marriage. Or maybe you've asked God to intervene but it feels as though he is absent or doesn't care enough to help. Why do I raise spirituality in a chapter on reclaiming fun and intimacy as a couple? Because for Carey and me, our faith was critical to our journey back to closeness and intimacy.

We were created to have a spiritual life. In the fall of 1987, someone explained to me that being a Christian isn't about practicing a religion but is about a relationship with the person of Jesus. Even before I had this life-changing conversation, I had started praying while walking to work in response to a prompting from who knows where. I found my fledgling faith bolstered by the eye-witness accounts written by people who did life with Jesus, such as the apostle John.[8]

People over the centuries have written about the value of faith in cultivating personal growth. Theologian John Calvin wrote, "Without knowledge of self there is no knowledge of God. Without knowledge of God there is no knowledge of self."[9] In other words, what you believe about yourself and what you believe about God are inextricably intertwined. I've found that to be true. Pursuing faith has led me to round out the offensive edges of my personality and work through painful emotional issues attached to my early-life trauma. It was my faith that led me to become more forgiving, because my heart was able to eventually agree with my mind that I'm not the judge. Knowing there's a God to whom I can entrust the responsibility of just judgment helps me separate myself from that role while preserving my peace of mind and sense of justice.

Our marriage has benefited from the love and power of Jesus in surprising ways. During the worst of our painful season, I attended a weekend conference and was feeling so emotional about the state of our marriage that I couldn't stay in the auditorium. I slipped out during one of the sessions, and for the next several hours, I drove around the back roads of the area and poured out my anger and tears to God. *Why, God? How could our marriage be such a mess? Do you even see my suffering? Do you even care?* My sense of entitlement surfaced too: *How could you lead me into a marriage like this when I've given up so much to serve you? How could you do this to me?*

A friend gave me a recording of the session I had missed and insisted I listen to it. When I did, the first recorded words I heard when I hit the button were these: "Jesus is enthralled by your beauty."[10]

Ever had a divine moment when you believe that something you hear, read, or see was meant just for you? This was one of those moments. I sat in stunned and silent awe. How could this be God's answer to me after all those hours I had raged at him? This message held no concrete answers or detailed explanations to my why and how questions. Yet God's clear answer was a simple, powerful affirmation of love: that he sees beauty in me despite myself. And this powerful moment brought healing to my soul and exposed some deep-seated self-loathing I hadn't yet faced.

What did this realization have to do with our struggling marriage? It was simple—if I didn't love myself, how could I truly love Carey? And if self-loathing was in me, even if my survival instincts had masked it, that would affect our closeness and intimacy. I believe the exact timing of those words was no accident or coincidence. It was too unlikely that the events would all line up, right down to my friend giving me a recording of the one conference session I missed, which was the one that I desperately needed to hear. Those words filtered into me at that precise time—a moment when it was clear I had not earned them, right after my fiercest rant at God. What Jesus spoke to me took laser-focused aim against the destructive but hidden belief in me that "I'm not lovable."

Those words that Jesus spoke to me in that moment are words he speaks to you. In his love for you, he is enthralled. Fascinated. Captivated. I really want for you to experience Jesus's kind of intimate love. Carey and I would both agree that growing in our intimacy with God helped us grow our intimacy with each other.

What does it take to have real intimacy between two people? A counselor I respect says to think of intimacy as "into-me-see."[11] In other words, to share an intimate relationship is to see deeply into each other and be exposed in an atmosphere of love, without fear or shame. When I know in my heart, not just in my mind, that God loves all of me as I am, unconditionally, it throws into sharp relief any unloving or loathing attitude I may have toward myself or my spouse. My faith has led me to recognize these negative attitudes as unspiritual and potentially destructive and to actively work on ridding myself of them.

Allowing our negative attitudes and beliefs to be exposed for what they are requires vulnerability and humility. Carey and I found that our individual journeys with Jesus helped us experience unconditional love and acceptance, even when we couldn't yet offer it to each other. Step by step, as I've grown in my faith, I've become a more loving partner for Carey. He's become a more loving version of himself as well.

Would Carey and I share the intimate connection we have today if we hadn't held tightly to our faith? We both say we wouldn't have stayed together without our faith. Ancient wisdom says, "A cord of three strands is not quickly broken."[12] At times, Carey and I were two broken strands. But Jesus was the third strand and the only one left intact, holding us together. And we're grateful for that, because now not only are we together but we're excited about being together more than ever before.

Would you be willing to take a step of faith? Are you curious about what it's like to have God breathe the breath of life into the parts of you or your marriage that are lacking life? If you are, then look at the people in your social circle. See if you know someone whose faith intrigues you. Invite this person for coffee or a walk and ask questions. Don't ask just the easy ones; bring up the ones that are keeping you skeptical about faith. Ask around your community to find a church that authentically loves people and makes you feel welcome when you walk through the door.

If you really want to dive into conversations about the difficulties you have with faith and Jesus, see if there's a program such as Alpha or Starting Point in your community. These are conversation-based programs that invite people to explore the authentic core beliefs of Jesus's followers. And as part of your exploration of faith, read the biblical book written by one of Jesus's closest disciples, John. If you want to know whether Jesus is real or not, just simply say, "Jesus, if you're real, please show me." When you pray this prayer, pay attention. In my experience, when someone prays this way and searches, God answers. I believe that God will answer you in a very individualized way so as to leave no doubt that the response is intended for only you.

There's space in these pages for you to breathe and be who you are. I'm not saying you have to try my version of faith to reclaim the fun and intimacy in your marriage, but I am saying that for Carey and me, our faith helped us grow closer and played a vital role in saving our marriage.

could you go from *that bad* to *this good*?

Don't give up on fun and intimacy. Chances are, one of you is more wired to drive fun in the moment, while the other is better at planning novel things to do together. Learn to appreciate and combine your individual strengths. Put your differences together so you can enjoy the whole package! Just because I'm not the first one people turn to when they're looking for a good laugh doesn't mean I won't surprise people with something funny here and there. Carey, on the other hand, is always looking for the latest funny video and often makes people laugh by doing or saying something goofy. We're a great one-two punch because while Carey is spontaneously fun, I'm the one who often sets the stage. I search out fun and novel experiences for us to share, and Carey's capacity to make fun in the moment makes even more of those experiences. When you think about how you and your spouse are wired, I bet the two of you could cook up some fun too.

Recently, Carey and I had a date night at home, complete with grilled Atlantic salmon and—my favorite—vanilla and lavender goat's milk ice cream. We laughed till it hurt. We shared our deeper thoughts from over the past couple of weeks. We were grateful, to the point that we gazed at each other through misty eyes. We could have been anywhere, eating burnt toast, and it wouldn't have dampened our fun. The point is that our time together *now* is so rich and filled with meaning and passion and fun because we had committed to not giving up and to moving step by step toward the relationship we aspired to.

It's your turn. I'm sure you can find exciting or novel activities to share. It may feel awkward to reclaim your sexual intimacy if it's fallen by the wayside, but I encourage you to reopen that conversation. It could end up being the best difficult conversation you've ever had. Replacing the tension in your marriage with some fun may help you focus on the inherent value in each other again. And if you explore spirituality, maybe you'll find more than you set out to look for.

FIND WHAT YOU *REALLY* WANT

1. Make a list of ten activities that seem novel or exciting to you and are realistic, given your availability and family circumstances. If your partner is willing, get him or her to make a list too. See if you can agree on four activities to try out together—maybe one each week for the next month or whatever schedule works for you both. Arrange childcare with family or friends.

2. Are you up to the challenge of a one-week criticism-free zone for your spouse? Yes, it's one-way (unless your spouse spontaneously decides to join in). During this week, focus on only your spouse's inherent value and positive qualities. Give compliments whenever you can do so sincerely.

3. How interested in physical intimacy would your partner say you are? How interested in physical intimacy do you think your partner is? If your sex life isn't where you want it to be, what is the best setting for an open and transparent conversation with your spouse about it?

CHAPTER 11

the company you keep

One day I was having coffee with a close friend. After listening to me complain about my marriage, she sensed I was stuck in a negative narrative. I had forced any balanced view of Carey's strengths and weaknesses through my own unidimensional, negative-focused filter. She saw what I couldn't see at the time: I wasn't appreciating his strengths or respecting the whole person of Carey.

After a while, my friend bravely confronted me with Carey's positive qualities. She talked about his loyalty, his heart for people, his dedication to his family, his gifts and talents, and his energy.

I was taken aback in the moment, but her words forced a crack through my negativity. Faced with her perspective, I started to see the deficiencies in mine.

Friends can be an amazing resource when you're going through marital struggles. Look around at your close friendships. Do you have a friend who will help you win in your marriage?

Our judgment is fallible. Our read of a situation isn't always accurate. We need friends who can help us see what we're blind to. We need friends who won't voice platitudes. It's important to confide in people who want the best for us and who have the courage to share their wisdom, not because it will make us feel good but because they hope to inspire us to do the next right thing. They're willing to deliver the harder message. They don't want "okay" for us—they want the best.

the wisdom of a good friend

Who will encourage and support you in taking a step to save your marriage?

Maybe you need a friend like Dave.

Dave has been married for more than a decade in his second marriage. He and his wife, Jennifer, each have two children, and they've invested a lot of time and energy to create a close-knit blended family and a thriving marriage.

He knew his friend Chris was in the middle of his kids' turbulent teenage years, feeling the distress of an unhappy marriage, and dealing with challenges at work. Chris couldn't help but feel the world was against him. After one particularly grueling week on the home front, Chris said, "That's it! I'm getting a divorce."

Dave spoke up. He didn't aim at a temporary fix for Chris's emotions. He leveled with him. "Divorce will be like a train wreck for your kids," Dave said. "Take it from me—I've been through it. At least for a time, it'll get *way* worse for you and your kids if you divorce. You have to exhaust every opportunity to stay together before you separate. Have you tried marriage counseling?"

Chris answered that he and his wife had tried counseling, but Dave wouldn't let him off the hook. "But have you *really* tried?"

Chris admitted that he felt put off by marriage counseling. "It's like two against one. They're always blaming me!"

Still, Dave pushed him further. "Have you accepted your share of the responsibility? Do you understand how you're contributing to the situation? Get a grip, and really work on it!"

Notice that Dave didn't voice platitudes, and he didn't shy away from being honest. He didn't say, "You seem to be at the end of your rope. You need a good workout—go pump some iron" or

"That's too bad" (followed by silence) or "You deserve better than this. Maybe it *is* time to move on." He challenged him to be open-minded and self-reflective and to question his own assumptions. He even took the risk of offending or angering him. He took a chance and pushed Chris to see what he wasn't seeing from his own perspective. Dave was being a friend by saying something Chris didn't want to hear but *needed* to hear.

After some time, Dave was glad to learn that Chris had reengaged with the counseling process. When Chris would complain, "Do you know how much this is costing me?" Dave would reply, "Do you know how much a divorce would cost?"

That was five years ago. Now Chris and his wife have been able to find deep satisfaction in their marriage. Chris tells anyone who will listen, "Dave saved my marriage." Both men see in retrospect the roles they played. Dave had the boldness to give wise advice to Chris when Chris's own decision-making would have led him down a painful path. Chris believes that had it not been for Dave's challenge to discover his own role in his marriage problems, he would have forgone the counseling and split. Because his marriage is now *this good,* Chris sees how much he would have lost if he'd isolated himself or surrounded himself with friends who said only what he wanted to hear. To his credit, Chris had the humility to listen to Dave and follow through by taking action and committing to the hard work. It paid off.

Find a wise friend like Dave. And when you're in the position to do it, be a friend like Dave.

"i don't need friends"

It's amazing how many people isolate themselves from the very help they need. In my work as a divorce attorney, an isolated spouse was a surprisingly frequent story. Sometimes when I helped clients negotiate their divorce settlements, their spouses' responses made no sense, but I often found that their spouses were going through the separation process with no meaningful support from anyone else. And the social isolation would show up as erratic behavior or irrational decisions during the separation proceedings.

A typical story went like this: "Over the years, my wife has grown distant from her family and friends. As a result, she doesn't really have anyone to turn to other than me. She refuses to see a counselor. And, of course, she doesn't want to hire a lawyer." Going through life lacking friends or confidantes had become normal for her. Sometimes mental-health problems and substance abuse were part of the picture. Being isolated was a symptom of a bigger problem: the spouse struggled to make and keep close relationships. Whatever was causing *that* had torn the fabric of the marriage.

Other than your spouse, is there another adult you share your successes, burdens, and secrets with?

In Western culture, now more than at probably any other time throughout history, we're at risk of being superficially connected but relationally isolated. The process of becoming isolated can be insidious; you may not see it happening. When a spouse becomes isolated, the impact on the marriage isn't positive. This is a truth Bob and Susan learned the hard way.

Bob and Susan are now happily married to each other—for a second time. Bob and Susan were high school sweethearts who both say they were happily married for a couple of decades while they raised their three children.

They had lived for several years in one community, where they were actively involved, and Bob had healthy, established friendships. But when Bob feared losing his job in their small suburb, he came up with a plan to relocate their family to a larger city a couple of hours away so he'd be able to find a job when the time came to look for one. The family moved. But Bob didn't lose his job after all, so he ended up commuting three to four hours every day to and from his workplace.

Since Bob was spending so much of his week driving and working, his time with his family became scarcer. Also, he didn't have the time or energy to invest in his new neighborhood. He lost touch with his old friends, and he didn't start building new relationships.

Once Bob realized how physically unhealthy his new commuting lifestyle was, he started walking for exercise during his lunch breaks. One of his work colleagues, Joanne, asked if she could join him. He didn't see a problem with them walking together, so he said yes.

Soon it seemed he was spending more time with Joanne on those walks than he was able to spend with his wife. Bob didn't set out to find a lover, but their walks eventually turned into an affair. The friends he'd once had would have held him accountable and talked to him about what he would be throwing away by leaving his marriage. But Bob had lost touch with his friends, and he had no one close to him except his new lover. He made the decision to divorce Susan quickly and without remorse.

Though, ultimately, how you react in your marriage is your responsibility, surrounding yourself with wise, trustworthy, and objective friends can help you make better decisions. You need these friends because you are not designed to carry the burdens of life by yourself. And your spouse is not designed to bear the weight of being your only friend.

After several years, Bob realized what he'd done and wholeheartedly confessed that he'd made a mistake in leaving Susan for another woman. He asked Susan for forgiveness shortly before he asked for her hand in marriage a second time, an offer she accepted. Bob admits that had he stayed connected to his friends, he might have avoided inflicting so much pain on his family. Susan forgave Bob more easily than he forgave himself.

Moving to a different city can obviously affect your relationships, but it's not the only way people become isolated these days. Social media can provide the feeling or illusion of connection while lacking realness and authenticity. Though we can have meaningful conversations with friends through social-media platforms, our friends don't usually get full disclosure on those platforms. Most people don't expose their deep secrets online, nor should we. Everyone has struggles they would rather not talk about, including things we may feel ashamed of. To make progress in personal growth, which ultimately affects marriage more than it does any other personal relationship, you actually do need to admit your weaknesses and real-life struggles to yourself and at least one other person—someone who will champion your marriage. Bringing our dark secrets into the light is an essential part of healing.

It's important to be an active part of a community. I'm not talking about your neighborhood or the locale you live in. I mean a community that consists of close and meaningful relationships with other adults, who may be friends, work colleagues, siblings, or parents. Community exists between people who are close enough emotionally to see each other for who they really are—strengths and weaknesses—and to be loved and accepted anyway. Community is absolutely necessary for all of us to grow and become the best versions of ourselves.

You may instinctively push back against this idea, but the truth is, you need unmasked, honest relationships with people who want the best for you.

And there's more. Not only do you need community, but you need community with people who will help you and hold you accountable. You can have friends, but they may not be the best for you or your marriage. Your choice of the company you keep matters.

beware the cheerleaders

Your friends will influence you to lean either *into* or *away from* your marriage. Research shows how much your marriage decisions are influenced by the people around you. In recent years, neuroscientific research has uncovered fascinating insights about how our brains respond to the influence of surrounding people. Moran Cerf, a neuroscientist and professor at Northwestern University, has done research into the social aspect of decision-making. Of Cerf's research, one reporter said,

> So long as we make the right choices, the thinking goes, we'll put ourselves on a path toward life satisfaction.
>
> Cerf rejects that idea. The truth is, decision-making is fraught with biases that cloud our judgment. People misremember bad experiences as good and vice versa; they let their emotions turn a rational choice into an irrational one; and they use social cues, even subconsciously, to make choices they'd otherwise avoid. . . .
>
> His neuroscience research has found that when two people are in each other's company, their brain waves will begin to look nearly identical.[1]

Cerf said, "This means the people you hang out with actually have an impact on your engagement with reality beyond what you can explain. And one of the effects is you become alike."[2]

Cerf's research findings don't strike us as counterintuitive; in fact, our life experiences have already taught us that people tend to rub off on one another. We become more like the people we keep company with.

When a marriage becomes difficult, if the norm among your friends or social circle is to get a divorce, then according to the research, divorce becomes a more likely outcome for you too.

Often the influence of others around us on whether to divorce and the myriad of decisions that must be made afterward seems more overt than the aligning of brain waves. Through the eyes of my clients, I've seen how friends and family do influence a couple as they move through the process of separating. So it's essential that you are aware of who you're allowing into your circle of influence.

"You go, girl!" is the rallying cry of friends, which I then heard repeated in my office by some of my clients who were soon-to-be divorced. Maybe you've heard stories like this: A spouse made new friends at the gym. An exercise class extended into drinks afterward. Then came the occasional party—first on weekends, then on weeknights as well. The spouse's life shifted from focusing on his or her family to focusing on losing weight, building muscle, improving his or her appearance, and socializing. These are not bad things in their rightful place, but when the marriage and kids get left behind, there's an obvious problem. And when the marriage is struggling, these friends are the ones who cheer their new pal toward "freedom."

Among the cheerleaders are friends who've gone through divorce already. They share war stories and plan out how their friend will "win." Cheerleaders chant messages that are reverberating throughout our culture, such as "Be strong—you're a warrior!" and "Take control of your life!"

Financial problems? Friends who've been through divorce can solve those too. They might say, "Take him for all he has" or "Bleed her dry." Cheerleaders help make the plan to leave the partner, to collect support payments, and to get maximum payments with the least inconvenience.

Parenting schedule problems? Cheerleaders strategize how to work the system to their friend's advantage. Sometimes they help frame allegations for court, even if they do stretch the truth a little. They coach their friend, saying things like, "If you make him mad and he gets physical, call the police and have him arrested. Then he'll be kicked out and placed under a restraining order, and you'll have the house and the kids."

You may think my view of cheerleaders is overly cynical, but this scenario happens more often than you think.

Who are the cheerleaders? They may be friends or disgruntled family members who were unhappy, right from the start, with their loved one's choice of a partner. Now they have their chance to help their loved one break free from this partner. Or the cheerleaders may be friends or work colleagues also going through divorces and looking for someone to commiserate with. Or it may be the "other" woman or man pushing for a divorce. The cheerleader may even be a friend of a friend, passing divorce advice along to anyone who will listen. Regardless, what you need to be aware of is that these people who give you advice with all the best of intentions may also be unaware that they're motivated to meet their own emotional needs in doing so. No, they aren't being selfish, and I'm not saying they are wrongly motivated. They may sincerely be trying to help you. But they're also possibly motivated by their own personal issues with your spouse or even their regrets from their own lives and marriages. Or they may just be looking for company as they journey through divorce with their own share of frustrations—they're looking for community with other people experiencing similar pain.

When you see breakups happening around you while your own marriage is struggling, it's natural to wonder whether divorce *is* the solution or maybe to believe that splitting is inevitable. Surrounded by divorce, it's easier to accept the circulating myth that humans were never intended to be monogamous. If you view healthy, monogamous marriage as being unattainable, as some would say, you'll tend to see the upsides of escaping your painful marriage, without seeing the downsides.

I know what it's like to have a divorce cheerleader pushing for influence. I had a close friend who insisted I needed to leave my marriage. When you're in emotional distress, you're more likely to give the cheerleaders' voices more power than they deserve.

The voices you listen to and the company you keep do matter. A lot. According to a recent study, "A person's tendency to divorce depends not just on his friends' divorce status, but also extends to his friends' friends."[3] This was no small study. These researchers used comprehensive social data collected from 5,124 people in seven data-collection waves from 1971–2001. The study was designed to zero in on the influence of friends on a person's divorce status.

Not surprisingly, these researchers concluded that divorce appears to occur in clusters. The people they studied were 75 percent more likely to divorce if a person they called a friend was divorced. The cluster influence wasn't significant for other connections, such as neighbor, coworker, or sibling. Researchers also found that divorce was 33 percent more likely if a friend of a friend was divorced. They concluded, "We suggest that attending to the health of one's friends' marriages might serve to support and enhance the durability of one's own relationship."[4]

I'm not saying you shouldn't be friends with people who are going through a divorce or have been divorced—far from it! But if your marriage is struggling, being deliberate about including people among your circle of friends who value marriage and want the best for *your* marriage is important.

Do the people around you (other than your spouse) help or hurt your marriage?

how do you find a good friend?

What if you don't have someone close to you who helps strengthen your marriage? How do you become part of a community that will help you save yours?

JOIN A MARRIAGE SUPPORT GROUP OR GO ON A MARRIAGE RETREAT

Let's say you've moved into a new community as Bob and Susan did and you'd like to make friends. You might look for friends by joining a club or fitness center or by volunteering. Or you might meet some neighbors while walking the dog. However, looking in these places for other couples who are passionate about having strong marriages may be hit-and-miss. It may be more effective to join a local marriage support group (find one through your local marriage counselor or community resource center) or go to a marriage retreat or workshop and network with other couples there. Organizations such as Imago Relationships and the Gottman Institute sponsor couples' workshops.[5] Finding an event or a group close to you will allow you the opportunity to learn ways to grow closer to your spouse while making friends with other couples who share your interest in building strong marriages.

JOIN A SMALL GROUP IN YOUR LOCAL CHURCH

Looking for these types of friendships in a healthy church is a wise strategy, even if you don't know what you believe about faith or you reject religion. How do you find a "healthy church"? After all, there are some unhealthy ones out there. When you find a church committed to loving the people in their neighborhood, you'll probably find great people who'll welcome you regardless of what you believe. Signs of a healthy church are people who seem to genuinely want to be there, to know Jesus better, and to help others. It's worthwhile to ask people you trust about a church's reputation.

Why look for friends in a church? Simply because it increases the chance you'll find people who also want their marriages to be strong. Many healthy churches have set up networks of small groups. These groups meet together regularly for mutual support, growth, and fun. A small group is often a mixture of couples and singles, but some churches may have groups dedicated to couples. If you're interested in a particular group, meet with them a few times to make sure the chemistry's good before you decide to join. Let the small-group leader know you're interested in getting to know other couples who value their marriages and you're looking to make some friends.

Belonging to a small group has been a huge benefit for Carey and me. We share our hopes, ideas, fears, struggles, and failings. We have confidence that the intimate things we share stay within the group. We have people to talk to when we mess up. We had friends in our small group rooting for our marriage to succeed when we were close to giving up. When we were struggling, these friends spent time encouraging and sometimes challenging us, like Dave did for Chris. These friends helped us see our next steps *and* our blind spots. They were great listeners, and they also helped us have fun sometimes, despite ourselves!

FIND AN EXPERIENCED COUNSELOR

Carey and I learned that sometimes we need help beyond what friends can provide. I know this has been my repeated refrain in this book, but please bear with me. If you find yourself lacking someone whom you can call at any time and share your honest struggles with, then you may be socially isolated. There's probably a reason that you're on your own, and for the sake of your marriage, find out why. As humans, we're not wired to do all our self-discovery and healing in isolation. Your past hurts involved others, and your healing will involve others too.

The advice Carey and I received in counseling was invaluable to the process of transforming our relationship. Our counselors helped us see how much our hurts from before our marriage drove the conflict we were mired in. After we got started with marriage counseling, making progress on one issue encouraged us to tackle other areas. Taking one step at a time in the same direction eventually transformed our marriage from very unhappy to thriving. In the end, we didn't regret a single minute, effort, or dollar we invested in getting professional advice to save our marriage.

Do your best to find professionals with a proven track record of helping unhappy couples. Invest time in reviewing the qualifications, experience, and feedback from other couples before you choose the professional to approach. Once you're in counseling, don't expect transformation to happen quickly—be patient and give it time.

Your employer may offer assistance benefits, including therapist or psychologist services. The pastor of your local church will likely be able to connect you with experienced marriage counselors or other resources. Our church maintains a vetted list of counseling professionals to refer people to and offers some financial help for counseling. Check to see if your local church provides these things too.

FIND AN ACCOUNTABILITY PARTNER

You're more likely to succeed if you make yourself accountable to someone else—preferably someone who shares your stated goals. During one podcast, pastor Albert Tate talked about how he and his small group of friends keep each other accountable for taking steps to build up their marriages, including keeping an active, healthy sex life.[6] Commit to honest disclosure with your accountability partner. Your friends can't help you if they don't know the truth about your struggles.

START SMALL

If you've been out of the habit of routinely making time to connect with friends, then start small and make sure the steps you take are a source of pleasure and not a burden for you. Whenever you decide to add a healthier habit to your life or try to get rid of a bad one, you're strategically better off if the change you make is small enough to allow you to easily succeed.[7] Maybe you're in the cynical place of "Who needs friends, anyway?" Let me be the Dave in your life and say to you, "*You* do. Don't let yourself off the hook. Whatever you do, don't stay isolated." Doing life with other people, even though it may sometimes get messy, offers moments of love and a source of strength that can't be replaced.

FIND WHAT YOU *REALLY* WANT

1. What does your choice of who you spend the most time with (other than your kids and work associates) say about how much you value wisdom?
2. Think of a time or two over the past year when an adult you're close to exposed one of your blind spots to you or cautioned you about something you weren't seeing clearly. How did you receive what he or she said?
3. If you are thinking about taking a next step toward rebuilding your relationship, talk to your spouse about planning a fun experience with another couple (or group of couples) you'd like to get to know better.

legacy: how your yes echoes into your (and your family's) future

What do you want the legacy of your marriage to be? Have you ever stopped to think about it? Starting today, what story are you writing in your future family's life? You've probably had the opportunity to observe how divorce has played itself out in multiple families. The choice you make today, either to split or to stay and work on your marriage, will affect you, your family, and even your community. You will leave a legacy. If you've never considered what your legacy will be—or even thought about why it's important—let me tell you about my friend Tina.

Tina was excited when her daughter Hannah decided to celebrate her personal faith by being baptized. As the celebration day approached, Tina's excitement crumbled into worry and despair because her divorced parents were going to attend the baptism. Almost two decades after their divorce, Tina's mom was still consumed with bitterness. She would not tolerate being in the same space as her ex-husband. Tina knew the slightest trigger was likely to emotionally set her off.

Rather than sharing Hannah's joy as they planned the event and after-party, Tina was wrapped up in the "Grandma SWAT plan"—brainstorming elaborate ways to whisk her mother in and out of rooms so that she wouldn't cross paths with Tina's father and his wife. The tentacles of Tina's mother's bitterness had wound themselves around not only her children but also her grandchildren.

Tina's story highlights how critical it is that you lift your eyes off your heartache to keep the long view of your family in focus.

Even if you don't have kids, your decision about whether to split or save your marriage is equally important. After all, what is the legacy of a strong long-term partnership of two people? If the marriage truly is all it can be, it stands as a testament to those laudable values many of us hold dear:

love

loyalty

steadfastness

perseverance

growth

humility

servant leadership

A long-term marriage that is healthy for both people lends life not only to the couple but also to others by its influence. It provides encouragement at just the right time for others who aspire to be longtime partners. Your efforts to write the qualities listed above into your own marriage story will see you enjoying their fruit, regardless of which course your relationship takes. Who knows? Maybe you will be able to rewrite the marriage story of your legacy.

As you consider splitting, surviving, or saving your marriage, I encourage you, especially when you're in a season of struggle, to put all your decisions through a legacy filter. Even the decisions that look more like split-second reactions or responses. Take the time to think through the legacy filter you choose. Your filter may look like one of these questions:

How will this shape my legacy?

What legacy am I about to leave by saying _____ or doing _____?

Am I leaving a legacy of respect or disrespect? Of honor or dishonor? Of generosity or scarcity? Of compassion or indifference?

Will _____ [an action, word, or attitude] leave my child a legacy of belonging to a *family* or a *broken family*? (Note: in drawing this distinction, I'm focusing on the strength of the family bonds and not whether or not each family member is living under the same roof.)

One problem you face when you go through a period of intense struggle or indifferent ambivalence is the blinding impact of emotional pain. Pain causes us to be self-focused and lose the ability to think about how today's choices may affect tomorrow's realities. Pain threatens to impede your progress toward what you really want for yourself, your marriage, and your family.

In exploring legacy, I want to share a few thoughts about overcoming three obstacles I've seen people trip over. How you handle these obstacles will affect your story and your children's stories too.

overcoming obstacle #1:
are you still growing?

I once met someone whose parents separated when she was a young child. I'll call her Rosetta. After the separation, Rosetta's mom snapped into survival mode. All the practical, real-life boxes had to be checked off: financial recovery, employment, a place to live, collecting belongings, moving furniture. The big box to check for Rosetta's mom was the long legal process to ensure Rosetta and her sister would live with her, not with her ex-husband.

Not ever stopping to grieve after her divorce, Rosetta's mother lugged the weights of anger and bitterness through her entire life. It was as if she had something to prove, like it was her, her daughters, and her cigarettes against the world. Instead of taking time to grieve, sharing her deep hurt with others, and searching for healing, Rosetta's mother leaned emotionally on her daughters. Yes, Rosetta and her mother maintained a close relationship that lasted. Yes, Rosetta grew up into a beautiful young woman who enjoys her work and has a healthy marriage of her own. (Rosetta largely credits her faith for that.) But thirty years after her parents' divorce, Rosetta was still coaxing and pleading with her mom to let it go.

When I was in the thick of our marriage despair, I was stuck in my own bitterness and needed help from a counselor to get out. As I delayed taking this step, my kids were missing out on the benefits of having an emotionally healthier mother. With the help of others, I realized that I needed to see myself and our circumstances from other perspectives. There were ways I needed to grow that I could not steer myself into. I needed to see isolation as my enemy, not as my friend.

You have the privilege of being able to think before you act, of pausing before responding. No one can take that away from you. Although personal growth and change require you to be persistent and accept some discomfort, you have the ability to choose how you respond to everything in your life, including your dinner that's burning, your neighbor who's being cranky, and your bitter feelings toward your spouse, who is being difficult.

If you peer inside and note that your emotions aren't what you want them to be, then don't pretend you don't see a problem. And don't waste your time being critical of yourself or turning your criticism on your spouse. But do ask yourself, *What do I need to do next?* and *When is my earliest opportunity to do it?* Make that step toward your healthier emotional life a high priority on your list. Do it without delay. Delay may only produce more incidents you would have preferred to avoid, more acts to later regret, and more angry words to feel guilty over. In short, nothing good is likely to come from delaying the steps you need to take to help yourself grow personally.

As Bob Goff, one of my favorite leaders, said,

> Things that go wrong can either shape us or scar us. I've had some things go well in my life, and some things not go so well, just like you. . . . And for me, I've realized that I used to be afraid of failing at the things that really mattered to me, but now I'm more afraid of succeeding at things that don't matter.[1]

There are any number of games, movies, shows, hobbies, and athletic pursuits that we tend to focus a lot of time on. Any of these pastimes may have their healthy place in our lives. But I raise the issue of time, wasting it or using it to succeed at things that don't matter, because I heard from so many clients who did not manage their internal strife or their marriage woes well—because they said they didn't have the time. People who needed to grow but wouldn't do so gave excuses that it would take too much energy, command too much time, and cost too much money.

I've been one of those people too at times. But as I see it now, none of these excuses makes sense. First, I am the only person who has to live with me 24-7 for the rest of my days. If I'm not emotionally healthy, then why wouldn't I pursue better health—not only for me but for my marriage, my children, my work, my friendships, and, frankly, my whole future? If I see a counselor and tell my story and am told that I don't have any real work to do, have I lost anything? And if I see a counselor who listens to my story and then points me toward the steps that will help me grow toward better emotional well-being, in the end I'm more likely to succeed in my marriage, my parenting, my work, and my other roles. Even from a financial perspective, the money I spend becoming emotionally healthy is money I'm likely to recover in the workplace anyway.

Commit to growing yourself. Because the truth is that as you become more emotionally healthy, you'll be better at connecting with not only your spouse but also your family, clients, employers, customers, colleagues, and friends.

overcoming obstacle #2:
you may not want your ex, but your children do

Maybe you know parents who are so locked in their battle that they can't see how their conflict is hurting their kids. Children who are exposed to extreme conflict between their parents are more likely as adults to develop physical or mental illnesses linked to that conflict.

Part of you may believe that your kids will be better off without the other parent's influence. It may be challenging to hear this, but your child really is better off with a close and meaningful relationship with each of you, whether or not you split.

Researcher Constance Ahrons elaborated on the effect of a divorce on the children, based on the level of cooperation between the parents. She studied 173 adults who were children when their parents separated approximately twenty years earlier. Their parents were divided into five categories based on their post-divorce relationship: "perfect pals," "cooperative colleagues," "angry associates," "fiery foes," and "dissolved duos" (no contact). Not surprisingly, "no single factor contributed more to children's self-reports of well-being after divorce than the continuing cooperative relationship between their parents."[2]

These adult children made it clear that they wanted their divorced parents to be cordial and not bad-mouth each other. They wanted to be able to share special occasions together, such as weddings and graduations. Adult children of parents who had hostilities were still caught up in loyalty conflicts. Some felt their lives were fragmented by having to keep their relationships with each parent separate. The children of hostile parents talked about the distress they felt trying to maneuver between parents and transition between homes.

Ahrons found that it was not uncommon for fathers to believe they had become unimportant in their children's lives. Based on her findings, she advocates for parents to recognize the importance of the father being an actively involved parent after their divorce. "What the findings point to," she wrote, "is that the ability of divorced parents to establish a supportive, low-conflict parental unit reverberates through the family even some twenty years later." This research also found that where parents still denigrated each other—even twenty years later—it was more likely that an adult child would withdraw from one or both parent relationships.[3]

Joan Kelly and Robert Emery studied 820 college students whose parents had separated when the students were children. They reported that 70 percent of the students would have preferred to live with both of their parents on a shared schedule after their parents' divorce.[4] Some students perceived that their caregiving parent was opposed to their spending time with their other parent, and they reported feeling more anger and being less close to their caregiving parent once they became adults. Both parents being substantially present in their children's lives after divorce protected the children's sense of well-being. Being raised by both parents was most likely important because it showed the children they were valued and loved.[5]

Your children need both of you. Your children need to see and perceive you and your spouse as cordial and cooperative. We all want the best for our kids! But let's be honest—we're still amateurs at building bonds, family life, and loving well. Home is where we *learn* to love. Regardless of the direction your marriage takes, do your best to reduce the conflict and work together in your parenting.

overcoming obstacle #3: the community your children belong to matters

You've probably heard the African proverb "It takes a village to raise a child." The saying is wise but not necessarily followed by our culture or justice systems in North America. Legally speaking, using the divorce process, parents have a good chance of being able to isolate their children from the influence of other adults if they are inclined to do so. As long as the kids are receiving an acceptable education, a judge is unlikely to intervene. Parents are permitted to shut out other important relationships, including those of loving grandparents, aunts, and uncles. Parents can move their kids from place to place to place, and no one will raise questions as long as there is no custody battle or child-protection case in progress.

Isolating kids is legally possible, but is it wise?

In *Parenting Beyond Your Capacity,* Reggie Joiner and my husband, Carey, made the case that one of the ways to help your children succeed is to guide them into meaningful relationships with other adults who will say the same things you, as a loving parent, would say. This is especially true as your kids grow and mature.

Reggie and Carey asked, "What are you doing to encourage your child's relationships with people outside the home?"[6] From Reggie's vast experience in working with children and teens, he wrote,

> I have observed a lot of teenagers. From the time they hit middle school, they start moving away from home. They

are not doing anything wrong; it's just the way they are made. They are becoming independent, and they begin redefining themselves through the eyes of other people who are not in their immediate family. The older they get, the more important it is for them to have other voices in their lives saying the same things but in a different way.[7]

When your kids hit the challenging teen years, you will discover you no longer have control as a parent. At that point, your kids may talk to another adult more readily and more openly than they will talk to you. It'll be better for your children to have the voices of other wise adults giving them direction instead of making their decisions alone or being guided by only their friends. Work to prevent your kids from being isolated from other positive adult influences. Think strategically about guiding your children toward a wise and loving community network, whether that includes extended family members, close and trusted friends, or vetted members of another community group or church.

the legacy of saying yes

I surveyed the open, brightly lit gym, the white walls and gleaming wood floors—well, mostly gleaming, except for the chalk dust shaken hastily off my teammates' hands. My eyes flitted over all the other gymnastics equipment that felt so familiar and inviting. I knew the excitement of springing off the mat and the fun of soaring over the vault, and I was up to the challenge of the beam. But from the bottom of one of the uneven bars, this was a new view—a scary one.

My right arm was outstretched behind my back, grasping the high bar for stability, and my toes were just visible as they hung off the bottom bar. I felt sweat leaching through the chalk dust on my hands. Nervously, I switched hands and swiped my right palm on the side of my thigh, attempting to wipe away my nerves at the same time. It didn't work. I shifted my weight from foot to foot and tried to avoid noticing my coach's furrowed brow. She was getting fidgety as the moments ticked by. After more of my shifting, nervous sighs, and false starts, she finally said, "This is the anchor move of your bar routine. You're not coming down till you jump."

But there was no guarantee about what would happen when I did. You see, she was asking me to launch myself backward over the top bar, free flying, and catch the bar on my way down. My entire body needed to fly backward over the bar in a V-shaped straddle. She could not stand near where I was, so I had no one to spot me or catch my fall. (My guess is there's currently way better equipment and safer methods since my days as a gymnast.) I could easily miscalculate my jump or miss the grasp on the bar once my feet were over. I might not clear the top bar with my feet or legs, and who knows what might break if I made that mistake. Without a doubt, the fall would be painful. It could even end my season. One failed takeoff or misaligned leg or weak grip and I would hit that faraway mat on the floor with momentum. And it was the flat mat, not the puffy one. If that happened, I'd forget all about my sweaty palms.

I stood on the bar long enough to feel a part of it. As my coach repeatedly sighed, watched the clock hands move, and glanced up at me from the floor, I weighed my options. For more than an hour. Several times, I almost jumped but backed down. Swallowing my nerves took so much effort. Perhaps my coach would have had more to say if she'd heard the battle inside my head. Something inside me said, *You need to give this a shot,* while another voice raised all the what-ifs. A third interrupted both of them: *If you do this—if you jump—you need to give it 100 percent.* I knew that any hesitation or half effort could be disastrous. I needed to be all in.

I don't recall exactly how the first and third voices drowned out the what-ifs. I jumped backward and cleared the top bar, and though it wasn't perfect, my grip was sure. My coach wasn't excited as much as she was intent on marking the moment so I would trust her judgment more readily the next time. And the clearest outcome for me was the exhilaration of that move. Flying freely over that bar turned out to be the best part of all the routines I competed with that year—routines that helped win medals and the county championships and took us as a team to the next level.

I had no idea how much rode on that moment as I stood on the bar, wrestling with my thoughts over a choice. I could have ultimately decided not to jump and accepted a safer routine with a lesser potential. But when I survey beyond my high school era to the rest of my life since then, I see this choice was preparing me. That moment of flying off the bar wasn't just about gymnastics; it was preparing me for all the other times I'd say an exhilarating yes.

Sometimes you're presented with a choice that calls you to move *past* your emotions because, let's be honest, your emotions (and mine) can be annoyingly stultifying.

I didn't know it then, but I believe other exhilarating experiences actually did hang in the balance that day on the bar. It was preparing me to say yes later, when I was at the top of the Matterhorn, about to tip my skis down; when I was trying to slalom water ski with my feet anchored in for the first time; and when I stood at a dizzying height on the high-ropes platform, just before making the swan dive to ring the bell. All these are thrilling moments I'm immensely grateful for. Each one forced me to ignore the fear rising in my chest and to quiet the what-ifs in the background. In retrospect, I can see that every one of these choices built on the previous one. They each led me one tiny step further along a path toward freedom from my self-limiting fear. You don't know how much freedom you might miss if you take a pass on risking a yes.

Consider what one best-case, realistic, successful outcome could look like, whether it be kicking the habit that's been dragging you down, finding a functional way through your marriage impasse, or searching for a way to forgive grievances and let go of bitterness. Then think about this: What if saying yes or no to taking a risky step to overcome this one problem could shape your approach to future problems? What if saying yes to this possibility of success opens a path toward other future possibilities—other experiences or successes that may be made possible only by saying yes now? Like saying yes to making that jump, with all the risk and no guarantees. But also saying yes to the possibility of an amazing result.

The way better future you aspire to have, the one you can start creating even if your spouse doesn't yet see the value, starts with you risking a yes. Maybe saying yes is finding an accountability partner. Maybe saying yes is circling a date on the calendar when you'll take the first step. Saying yes moves you forward even when your emotions urge you to freeze or back down. Remember your three options for your marriage: split, survive, or save. What is it that you *really* want? As you weigh the options and listen to wise advice, I do want you to prepare yourself to say yes to one step in the direction of positive personal growth. In which dimension of your overall well-being do you find your most pressing priority for growth? Physical? Emotional? Spiritual? Financial? Relational? Don't make it overwhelming, because the path to get you from here to there doesn't need to be. Your path to a way better future consists of a series of tiny but determined baby steps, one at a time. Just one yes, followed by one step, one at a time.

What is the one step you'll say yes to? Is there something in your behavior or your life that you and your spouse would be better off without? What challenging question about your life choices do you imagine your children may ask you when they're older? If you can identify just one next step toward building a stronger marriage or deeper bonds with your kids, will you risk saying yes?

Even if getting to yes leaves you shifting to find your balance, hear me as your coach: Don't come down till you jump. Take that next step. The one that feels risky to you. The one that predicts a chance of a positive outcome. With no strings attached, give something you know is important to your spouse. Be generous with your time. Start doing the thing your spouse has been begging you to do. Pick up the phone, call someone close to you, and ask for help. Accept an invitation to attend a support group. And as you jump, throw your whole weight into it. A half-hearted effort will only sell you and your loved ones short or land you in a heap. Once you've decided to say yes, go all in.

And when you've taken that first step, say yes again and again, and as you move along from one step to the next, capture them so you can trace them out later. And someday you'll marvel at how the exhilaration of saying yes has echoed into your future.

FIND WHAT YOU *REALLY* WANT

1. Identify a legacy-filter question, such as those on page 177, that resonates with you. Try running your relationship, parenting, and time-prioritizing decisions through this filter over the next seventy-two hours. Notice whether the legacy-filter question shifts the way you make these decisions. After your trial run, take time to re-evaluate and maybe try it again with a different question.

2. Ask a trusted friend, "What area of my emotional or mental health do you think may be holding me back?"

3. What single step toward your own personal growth holds the most risk—requiring you to overcome your fears and go all in—but offers the potential of life-altering reward? (If you need help figuring out your next step, you can find helpful tools and resources at www.toninieuwhof.com.)

acknowledgments

I've said it takes a village to raise a marriage, and now I know that it takes one to create a book about marriage too. For every individual, beyond those mentioned here by name, who's influenced the shaping of this book, I'm profoundly grateful. This book wouldn't be the same without you.

To my husband, Carey. Where do I even start? When I said forever to "us," I had no idea what was to come. You are the person who has loved me the most. You are the love of my life, my biggest fan, my best friend, a mentor, and, to top it off, my personal in-house comedian. Your encouragement and energy spur me on. Your skillful editing has made this book more than it would have been. I wouldn't trade the world for all the laughs, love, hardships, and tears we've been through, and there aren't enough words to express the gratitude I feel for you and our marriage. No doubt you are God's abundant blessing for me.

To my sons, Jordan and Sam, you always have brought me joy, softened my heart, and inspired me to be a better human—and still do. I'm grateful for your support and feedback during this book project, as well as for your insightful approaches to life in general. Thank you for trusting me with your deep thoughts.

To Emily Newton, you are a jewel, and it has been my joy and privilege to get to know you better. For your support with creative ideas and feedback, as well as with the book-review event, I am thankful.

For the support of Connexus Church and all the people who have shared their lives with us in our small groups over the years, thank you for keeping the faith and helping us through. To Brenda and John MacFadyen, Rose and Rob Meeder, Anita and Brad Perrigo, and Maria and Edward Chafe, I'm grateful for the privilege of doing life with you during this season and for how you've buoyed my spirits to carry me along this book-writing process. To Jeff and Leslie Brodie, your leadership has been an encouragement to me and is making this world a better place. Jeff Brodie and Christine Birch, I'm grateful that you made space for me at the Connexus volunteer conference to survey our members about marriage and learn more about their challenges. The messages in these pages have shifted as a result.

Rose Meeder, just by the way you live and love, you've pushed me to get out of my head and into the world. You inspire me, my friend! Thank you for your invaluable feedback during this process. Lynn Kirwin, my dear friend who is never afraid to stand up against injustice, I value your impact on my life. You keep me moving—literally!—and I appreciate that you shared your expertise to form these messages. To Sarah Piercy, what started off as a professional relationship has morphed into much more, and I always value what you draw out of your well of sound judgment and creativity, and even better, I value the love you so freely share. To Ali Gentry, you are filled with wisdom beyond your years and you live life to the full. Even though you are pouring out your gifts into the world, much in demand, you've carved out the time to be a dear friend—praying, supporting, and providing feedback along the way—and I am thankful beyond words.

I want to thank my parents, Audrey and Dave Karsikas, and Carey's parents, Marja and Marten Nieuwhof, for your steadfast presence in our family's lives. I'm grateful for your unwavering faith and your support for all of us. As well, I'd love to thank our siblings and extended family members for your gracious interest and words of encouragement as this book went from idea to proposal to manuscript.

To our counselors, Dr. Jim Sitler, Dr. Craig Brannan, and Alf Davis, without your influence, skill, and words of wisdom, I'm not sure where our marriage would be now. We are indebted.

To the leaders who have made personal sacrifices to share their gifts with the world so that my path, ability to speak up, and personal formation are different as a result, I am grateful more than you know: Danielle Strickland, Ann Voskamp, Christy Wimber, Jon Acuff, Donald Miller, Dr. Terry Wardle, Andy and Sandra Stanley, Jeff and Wendy Henderson, Bob and Maria Goff, and Reggie and Debbie Joiner.

To Lysa TerKeurst and the COMPEL team, your enthusiasm and invaluable guidance during our team's time with you has ended up shaping these messages, and I would be remiss not to mention the impact you've had on me. I'm excited for the mission you're on!

To Brian Galbraith and beautiful Nicole, you believed in me more than I believed in myself, and without your invitation for me to join your team, this book could not exist. Brian, your mentoring is impactful and your optimism is contagious, and these have been true gifts to me.

When I said it takes a village, I really meant it. To Linda Paisley, David Cavon, Michael and Shelley Unwin, Justin and Amber Morton, Mark and Joanna Faris, Justin Piercy, Karen and Erik Snow, Hillary Klassen, Roslyn and Anton Lim, Gary Hurst, Carly Bartlett, Mary Dyck, and Dawn Richmond, I extend my sincere thanks for sharing your stories and thoughts. Each one of you I deeply respect and have so valued your input. For the counseling and coaching professionals and their spouses who shared their wealth of wisdom and learning in their areas of expertise on these topics, I am truly grateful: Dr. Craig and Rene Brannan, Dr. Larry and Sharon Pardy, Em and Marc Dyson, and Jordan and Alicia

Mason. And for my fellow Connexus team members whose support has been invaluable to me: Jenn Konrad, Doris Schuster, Kelley Wright, and Marie Metsa.

And last but certainly not least are all the wonderful people from the publishing world whom I'm indebted to. To Esther Fedorkevich, I am certain this book wouldn't exist without you. Your tenacity was a key motivator, and your clear belief in this message prompted me to take your invitation seriously. Whitney Gossett, thank you for your focused guidance and all the skill you've lent to this book process along the way. Thank you to the whole Fedd Agency team—you are amazing! To Ginger Kolbaba, you've been oh so patient in helping to shape, enrich, and fortify the words on these pages. Thank you for sharing your brilliance with me and us! To Susan Tjaden, you've provided the guiding light throughout this book-writing journey and have done so much to bring clarity and order to this messaging. And also to Andrew Stoddard, Laura Barker, Johanna Inwood, Brett Brenson, and the whole WaterBrook team, thank you for your invaluable support and for taking a chance on someone so green to publishing.

notes

CHAPTER 1: IS THERE REALLY NO WAY OUT OF STUCK?

1. A quick side note: Now that I've mentioned I'm married to a pastor, I've raised the matter of faith. Maybe you don't believe what I believe, and that's okay. Please know there's breathing room in these pages for what you believe. Even if you and I don't see everything eye to eye, let's forge ahead through these messages together, because I want something *for* you.

CHAPTER 2: "IT'S NOT MY FAULT"

1. It's important for you to know that my relationship with my parents has changed. I love my parents, and I appreciate the ways they've grown over the years. I've heard it said that you can't expect out of someone what was never put into them in the first place. I believe this is true of my parents as well. I couldn't expect an emotionally healthy upbringing from my parents since they hadn't experienced it themselves. For more thoughts on this idea, listen to Sam Collier in "Sam Collier on Growing Up Without Privilege, Living a Double Life, Boundaries for Difficult People and How to Build Influence," *Carey Nieuwhof Leadership Podcast,* episode 203, July 16, 2018, https://careynieuwhof.com/mypodcast/.

2. Jeff Henderson, *Climate Change* (Alpharetta, GA: Northpoint Resources), DVD series, https://northpoint.org.

3. For more insight into how to create new habits and implement behavior change, read James Clear's book, *Atomic Habits: An Easy and Proven Way to Build Good Habits and Break Bad Ones* (New York: Avery, 2018).

CHAPTER 3: "I'M NOT BEING UNREALISTIC, RIGHT?"

1. Ann Wilson and Dave Wilson, *Vertical Marriage: The One Secret That Will Change Your Marriage* (Grand Rapids, MI: Zondervan, 2018), 221–25.

2. John Gottman, "The Truth About Expectations in Relationships," Gottman Institute, January 30, 2018, www.gottman.com/blog /truth-expectations-relationships/.

3. "Plans fail for lack of counsel, but with many advisers they succeed" (Proverbs 15:22).

4. Andy Stanley, "What Happy Couples Know, Part 1: Nothing // Andy Stanley," YouTube video, 40:13, January 29, 2018, https:// youtube.com/watch?v=ARc8ye08JXc.

CHAPTER 4: SPLIT, SURVIVE, OR SAVE: WHAT DO YOU REALLY WANT?

1. Gary Hurst, conversation with author, November 10, 2018.

2. Registered social workers Em Dyson and Larry Pardy and counselor/coach Jordan Mason.

3. Learn more about the power of vulnerability from a leading expert: Brené Brown, *Daring Greatly: How the Courage to Be Vulnerable Transforms the Way We Live, Love, Parent, and Lead* (New York: Avery, 2015).

4. Bianca P. Acevedo et al., "Neural Correlates of Long-Term Intense Romantic Love," *Social Cognitive and Affective Neuroscience* 7, no. 2 (February 2012): 145–59, https://academic.oup.com/scan/article /7/2/145/1622197.

5. Linda J. Waite et al., "Does Divorce Make People Happy?," Institute for American Values (New York: Institute for American Values, 2002), http://americanvalues.org/catalog/pdfs/does_divorce _make_people_happy.pdf.

CHAPTER 5: HOW TO MOVE CLOSER INSTEAD OF MOVING ON

1. This conference was over three decades ago, so I don't recall the name of the physician or the conference, but the quote is the gist of what he said.

2. For more information, see Daniel Goleman, *Emotional Intelligence: Why It Can Matter More Than IQ* (New York: Bantam Books, 2005).

3. Dr. Sue Johnson, *Hold Me Tight: Seven Conversations for a Lifetime of Love* (New York: Hachette Book Group, 2008), 134–38.

4. These examples are adapted from Dr. Timothy Lane, "Marriage and Emotional Intelligence," *Tim Lane and Associates* (blog), September 5, 2017, http://timlane.org/blog/marriage-and-emotional -intelligence. Used by permission. All rights reserved.

5. Lewis B. Smedes, *Forgive and Forget: Healing the Hurts We Don't Deserve,* 2nd ed. (New York: Harper One, 2007), 27–30.

6. Desmond Tutu and Mpho Tutu, *The Book of Forgiving: The Fourfold Path for Healing Ourselves and Our World* (New York: HarperOne, 2014), 129–31.

CHAPTER 6: STOP FIGHTING! HOW TO MAKE PEACE, STARTING NOW

1. For more about the victim story and how to expose it to successfully navigate difficult conversations, read Kerry Patterson et al., *Crucial Conversations: Tools for Talking When Stakes Are High,* 2nd ed. (New York: McGraw-Hill Education, 2012), 116–17.

2. John Gottman and Nan Silver, *The Seven Principles for Making Marriage Work: A Practical Guide from the Country's Foremost Relationship Expert* (New York: Harmony Books, 2015), 116.

CHAPTER 7: YOUR CONFLICT AFFECTS YOUR KIDS MORE THAN YOU REALIZE

1. "Court Conjures 'Breaking Bad' Analogy for Warring Parents," FamilyLLB Ontario Divorce Education Centre, October 31, 2016, https://familyllb.com/2016/10/31/court-conjures-breaking-bad -analogy-for-warring-parents; an Ontario judgment in the public

domain, [2014] ONSC 4002, www.canlii.org/en/on/onsc/doc /2014/2014onsc4002/2014onsc4002.html.

2. For more on healthy parenting approaches to forming strong bonds with your kids, try starting with one of the following: Gary Chapman and Ross Campbell, *The 5 Love Languages of Children: The Secret to Loving Children Effectively* (Chicago: Northfield, 2012); Adele Faber and Elaine Mazlish, *How to Talk So Kids Will Listen and Listen So Kids Will Talk* (New York: Harper Perennial, 2002); Ross W. Greene, *Raising Human Beings: Creating a Collaborative Partnership with Your Child* (New York: Simon and Schuster, 2016); Daniel Siegel and Tina Payne Bryson, *The Whole-Brain Child: 12 Revolutionary Strategies to Nurture Your Child's Developing Mind* (New York: Bantam Books, 2012); Daniel Siegel and Tina Payne Bryson, *No-Drama Discipline: The Whole-Brain Way to Calm the Chaos and Nurture Your Child's Developing Mind* (New York: Bantam Books, 2014).

3. JoAnne Pedro-Carroll, *Putting Children First: Proven Parenting Strategies for Helping Children Thrive Through Divorce* (New York: Avery, 2010).

4. Reid Wilson and Lynn Lyons, *Anxious Kids, Anxious Parents: 7 Ways to Stop the Worry Cycle and Raise Courageous and Independent Children* (Deerfield Beach, FL: Health Communications, 2013), 17.

5. Sissy Goff, *Raising Worry-Free Girls: Helping Your Daughter Feel Braver, Stronger, and Smarter in an Anxious World* (Minneapolis: Bethany, 2019), 52.

CHAPTER 8: WHERE COULD STEPS OF FORGIVENESS TAKE YOU?

1. Desmond Tutu and Mpho Tutu, *The Book of Forgiving: The Fourfold Path for Healing Ourselves and Our World* (New York: HarperOne, 2014), 223.

2. If your partner has had an affair, please know that I feel the heaviness of sorrow for you even as I write these words. Authors have devoted entire books to this particularly painful type of betrayal, and I encourage you to seek the benefits of their insight and wisdom: Shirley Glass, *NOT "Just Friends": Protect Your Relationship from Infidelity and Heal the Trauma of Betrayal* (New York: Atria, 2004); Mira Kirshenbaum, *I Love You but I Don't Trust You: The*

Complete Guide to Restoring Trust in Your Relationship (New York: Berkley Books, 2012); Janis Abrahms Spring, *After the Affair: Healing the Pain and Rebuilding Trust When a Partner Has Been Unfaithful* (New York: William Morrow, 2012); Michele Weiner-Davis, *Healing from Infidelity: The Divorce Busting Guide to Rebuilding Your Marriage After an Affair* (Boulder, CO: Michele Weiner-Davis Training Corp, 2017).

3. Lewis Smedes, *Forgive and Forget: Healing the Hurts We Don't Deserve,* 2nd ed. (New York: HarperCollins,1996), xix.

4. Dr. Martin Luther King Jr., *Strength to Love* (Minneapolis: Fortress, 2010), 44–45.

5. Tutu and Tutu, *Book of Forgiving,* 142.

6. Dr. Charity Byers, Blessings Ranch, conversation with author, January 16, 2020.

7. Spring, *After the Affair,* 84–85.

8. For more on forgiveness, these are a good place to start: Tutu and Tutu, *Book of Forgiving;* Gary Chapman and Jennifer Thomas, *When Sorry Isn't Enough* (Chicago: Northfield, 2013); Smedes, *Forgive and Forget*.

CHAPTER 9: DON'T PLAY IT SAFE

1. *Wonder Woman* (Burbank, CA: Warner Bros), 2017.

2. If you have questions about your actual safety, then you need to create safe boundaries. I'm *not* encouraging you to throw caution to the wind if you're in harm's way.

3. Gary Chapman, *The 5 Love Languages: The Secret to Love That Lasts* (Chicago: Northfield, 2015). Take an online assessment to discover your love language at www.5lovelanguages.com.

4. Henry Ford, www.thehenryford.org. Original quotation from *Ford News,* June 1, 1922, 2.

5. *Christopher Robin* (Burbank, CA: Walt Disney Studios), 2018.

6. *Merriam-Webster,* s.v. "tenacity," www.merriam-webster.com /dictionary/tenacity.

7. Psalm 126:6.

8. Nicky and Pippa Gumbel talk about this in their Bible commentary: *The Bible in One Year: A Commentary,* May 9, Day 129, www.bibleinoneyear.org/bioy.

CHAPTER 10: FIND THE FUN AND INTIMACY
YOU'VE BEEN MISSING

1. Kimberley Coulter and John Malouff, "Effects of an Intervention Designed to Enhance Romantic Relationship Excitement: A Randomized-Control Trial," *Couple and Family Psychology: Research and Practice* 2, no. 1 (2013): 34–44, https://psycnet.apa.org/doiLanding?doi=10.1037%2Fa0031719; Charlotte Reissman, Arthur Aron, and Merlynn Bergen, "Shared Activities and Marital Satisfaction: Causal Direction and Self-Expansion Versus Boredom," *Journal of Social and Personal Relationships* 10, no. 2 (May 1, 1993): 243–54, https://journals.sagepub.com/doi/10.1177/026540759301000205.

2. Henry Cloud and John Townsend, *21 Days to a Great Marriage: A Grownup Approach to Couplehood* (Nashville: Thomas Nelson, 2006), 52.

3. John Gottman, *The Science of Trust: Emotional Attunement for Couples* (New York: Norton, 2011), 266.

4. John Gottman and Nan Silver, *The Seven Principles for Making Marriage Work: A Practical Guide from the Country's Foremost Relationship Expert* (New York: Harmony Books, 2015), 22, 67–86.

5. Brent J. Atkinson, *Emotional Intelligence in Couples Therapy: Advances from Neurobiology and the Science of Intimate Relationships* (New York: Norton, 2005), 82.

6. Carey Nieuwhof spoke about the concepts in this section in a message titled "Part 3: Forgotten Masterpiece" as part of the Enneagram sermon series at Connexus Church, January 26, 2020, https://connexuschurch.com/sermon/forgotten-masterpiece/.

7. For more insight on how to rebuild a loving, strong connection, I recommend Gary Chapman, *The 5 Love Languages: The Secret to Love That Lasts* (Chicago: Northfield, 2015); Cloud and Townsend, *21 Days to a Great Marriage;* Gottman and Silver, *Seven Principles for Making Marriage Work;* Dr. Sue Johnson, *Hold Me Tight: Seven Con-*

versations for a Lifetime of Love (New York: Hachette Book Group, 2008); Howard J. Markman et al., *12 Hours to a Great Marriage: A Step-by-Step Guide for Making Love Last* (San Francisco: Jossey-Bass, 2003).

8. See the book of John in the Bible.

9. John Calvin, *The Knowledge of God the Creator,* Center for Reformed Theology and Apologetics, https://reformed.org/books/institutes/books/book1/bk1ch01.html.

10. This statement is adapted from Psalm 45:11, and it relies on the imagery described by King David as he envisioned the messianic king (foreshadowing Jesus Christ) and described the bride (foreshadowing the bride of Christ, the body of believers).

11. Craig Brannan, PhD, Next Step Counselling, conversation with author, August 29, 2019.

12. Ecclesiastes 4:12.

CHAPTER 11: THE COMPANY YOU KEEP

1. Chris Weller, "A Neuroscientist Who Studies Decision-Making Reveals the Most Important Choice You Can Make," *Business Insider,* July 28, 2017, www.businessinsider.com/neuroscientist-most -important-choice-in-life-2017-7.

2. Moran Cerf, quoted in Weller, "Neuroscientist Who Studies."

3. Rose McDermott, James Fowler, and Nicholas Christakis, "Breaking Up Is Hard to Do Unless Everyone Else Is Doing It Too: Social Network Effects on Divorce in a Longitudinal Sample," *Social Forces 92,* no. 2 (December 2013): 491–519, https://academic.oup .com/sf/article-abstract/92/2/491/2235848?redirectedFrom=fulltext.

4. McDermott, Fowler, and Christakis, "Breaking Up."

5. For more information about these ministries, see https://imago relationships.org and www.gottman.com.

6. Albert Tate, "Albert Tate on How to Add Humour to Your Talks, a Conversation About Porn and Sex, and Handling the Pressures of Leadership," *Carey Nieuwhof Leadership Podcast,* episode 301, No-

vember 6, 2019, https://podcasts.apple.com/ca/podcast/carey
-nieuwhof-leadership-podcast-lead-like-never-before/id912753163
?i=1000456115919.

7. For more on this idea, listen to "James Clear—How to Hack Your Habits to Achieve Lasting Change," *Building a StoryBrand with Donald Miller,* podcast, episode 175, https://podcasts.apple.com/ca /podcast/building-a-storybrand-with-donald-miller/id1092751338?i =1000457104663, or read James Clear's book, *Atomic Habits: An Easy and Proven Way to Build Good Habits and Break Bad Ones* (New York: Avery, 2018).

CHAPTER 12: LEGACY: HOW YOUR YES ECHOES INTO YOUR (AND YOUR FAMILY'S) FUTURE

1. Bob Goff, *Love Does: Discover a Secretly Incredible Life in an Ordinary World* (Nashville: Thomas Nelson, 2012), 30.

2. Constance Ahrons, "Family Ties After Divorce: Long-Term Implications for Children," *Family Process,* 58, https://onlinelibrary .wiley.com/doi/abs/10.1111/j.1545-5300.2006.00191.x.

3. Ahrons, "Family Ties," 58.

4. Joan B. Kelly and Robert E. Emery, "Children's Adjustment Following Divorce: Risk and Resilience Perspectives," *Family Relations* 52, no. 4 (2003): 352–62, https://psycnet.apa.org/record/2003 -09485-005?psychLogin:logi342=Log%20In&psychLogin=psych Login.

5. Kelly and Emery, "Children's Adjustment," 359.

6. Reggie Joiner and Carey Nieuwhof, *Parenting Beyond Your Capacity: Connect Your Family to a Wider Community* (Colorado Springs, CO: David C Cook, 2010), 64.

7. Joiner and Nieuwhof, *Parenting Beyond Your Capacity,* 66.

Toni Nieuwhof is an author, speaker, and family law mediator and has spent decades of her professional life practicing law and combining her professional careers of pharmacist and lawyer in leadership roles for hospitals. Her most challenging work as a lawyer involved advising and representing people going through the journey of divorce. In her roles as a mediator and a lawyer, she is a steadfast voice for the well-being of the children involved.

Toni cofounded and cohosts the *Smart Family Podcast* to help people love being home (www.smartfamilypodcast.com). You can connect with Toni on Instagram at @toninieuwhof, on Facebook at Toni Karsikas Nieuwhof, and on her website at www.toninieuwhof.com. Toni and her husband, Carey Nieuwhof, started one of North America's most influential churches near Barrie, Ontario, where they currently reside.

ABOUT THE TYPE

This book was set in Bembo, a typeface based on an old-style Roman face that was used for Cardinal Pietro Bembo's tract *De Aetna* in 1495. Bembo was cut by Francesco Griffo (1450–1518) in the early sixteenth century for Italian Renaissance printer and publisher Aldus Manutius (1449–1515). The Lanston Monotype Company of Philadelphia brought the well-proportioned letterforms of Bembo to the United States in the 1930s.

Because Home Isn't Always
What You Thought It Would Be

Get high-quality, practical advice to help you strengthen your marriage and boost your parenting to the next level.

Tune in to the **Smart Family Podcast,** *available on all the podcast platforms, or visit us at smartfamilypodcast.com.*

Get the tools you need to take the next steps toward your Way Better Future:

- Accountability plan
- Way Better Future map
- Other tools and resources

Visit toninieuwhof.com to learn more.